Keep Your
Outboard Motor
Running

Keep Your Outboard Motor Running

Richard Thiel

Distributed by:
Airlife Publishing Ltd.
101 Longden Road, Shrewsbury SY3 9EB, England

*To my father, who kept nagging me to follow directions
and pick up my tools.*

Published by International Marine
10 9 8 7 6 5 4
Copyright © 1992 International Marine, a division of The McGraw-Hill Companies.

All rights reserved. The publisher takes no responsibility for the use of any of the materials or methods described in this book, nor for the products thereof. The name "International Marine" and the International Marine logo are trademarks of The McGraw-Hill Companies. Printed in the United States of America.

Library of Congress Cataloging-in-Publication Data
Thiel, Richard, 1945–
   Keep your outboard motor running / Richard Thiel.
     p.   cm.
   Includes index.
   ISBN 0-87742-328-8
   1. Outboard motors—Maintenance and repair.   I. Title.
VM771.T44 1992
623.8'7234'0288—dc20   92-12665
                                   CIP

Questions regarding the content of this book should be addressed to:

International Marine
P.O. Box 220
Camden, ME 04843

Questions regarding the ordering of this book should be addressed to:
The McGraw-Hill Companies
Customer Service Department
P.O. Box 547
Blacklick, OH 43004
Retail customers: 1-800-822-8158
Bookstores: 1-800-722-4726

Text design by Faith Hague, Watermark Design, Camden, Maine.

CONTENTS

Introduction

The purpose of this book is to give you a brief and painless explanation of how your outboard propulsion system works, plus provide some simple operational and maintenance guidelines that will ensure you get maximum life and durability from it. Once you understand the basics provided here, you'll be able not only to devise your own strategies and programs, but also to deal intelligently with a mechanic when you need one.

This book is written for someone who knows absolutely nothing about engines and things mechanical and, equally important, someone who has little or no interest in them other than making sure they serve him well. In short, this is a basic survival manual for the owner of a boat equipped with an outboard.

This book is not about the history of outboard development, how to conduct major repairs, or how to rebuild an engine or drive unit in your bedroom using just a hammer and screwdriver. In fact, you'll find few, if any, references to actual repair procedures here. Instead, the emphasis is on getting the best use out of your outboard and preventing problems from occurring in the first place.

Why? Because in spite of what you may have read or heard to the contrary, the modern outboard propulsion system is a surprisingly simple and reliable piece of machinery. Throughout its life it rarely needs major work or attention. But when it does, unless you are a person of exceptional mechanical ability and have access to a large assortment of specialized tools, you'll be far better off leaving significant repairs to someone who not only has the tools, but the extensive specialized training in the art (yes, art) of troubleshooting and repairing an outboard propulsion system.

The outboard's admirable reliability springs directly from its simplicity. As we'll see, the outboard powerhead, which is the engine portion, typically has about half the parts of the comparable four-cycle engine, such as that found in a stern drive or automobile. In addition, it has no circulating lubrication system. This means it is easy to maintain and repair, as well as durable, light, and reliable.

Moreover, the drive unit portion of the outboard, that which takes power from the powerhead and transmits it to the propeller, is also simple and reliable, having been proved in decades of use. Consequently, if you operate and maintain your outboard properly you should have years of trouble-free operation ahead of you before you have to call a mechanic.

In addition to learning the basics of engine and drive unit operation, this book will help you choose the spare parts and tools you should have aboard at all times, regardless of the size of your boat or where you take it. Fortunately only a few tools and parts are really necessary, but having them can make the difference between a cruise that leaves you with fond memories and one that leaves only woeful regrets.

Finally this book will provide you with a basic introduction to the art of troubleshooting, a skill that not only allows you to fix the minor problems that inevitably crop up on even the best-maintained engine, but one that enables you to deal intelligently with the person you hire to fix the big ones. By applying the time-proven principles of troubleshooting and the basic working knowledge of the outboard power system you will have gleaned from the first chapters of this book, you will—believe it or not—be able to reason through most maladies before having to call an expert.

Outboards are expensive and so are mechanics. A good marine mechanic—if you can find one—typically will charge $40 an hour and more, and it takes a lot of time to work on an outboard. Add to that the fact that marine parts cost usually half-again as much as automotive parts and you have good reason to get as much trouble-free performance out of your boat and outboard as you can.

This shouldn't be cause for alarm. The good news is that if properly operated and maintained the typical two-cycle outboard engine can last at least as long as the boat to which it was mounted. And the drive unit portion is at least as durable. The key to durability is to make sure you minimize wear by operating and maintaining your outboard properly.

Giving you a working knowledge that will allow you to maximize the trouble-free life of your outboard is what this book is all about.

One note before we start: The vast majority of outboards on the water today use what's called the two-stroke cycle. (We'll explain it in a later chapter.) Although there are some four-cycle outboards on the water, manufactured mainly by Yamaha and Honda, they make up only a small percentage of the overall outboard population. Therefore, for the purposes of this book, we will assume that all outboards use the two-stroke cycle.

PART ONE

How the Outboard Works

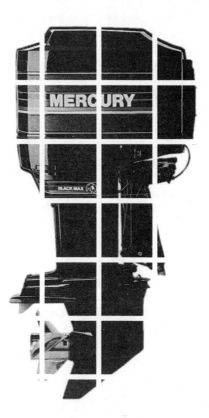

The Internal Combustion Engine

The gasoline engine that powers your outboard has little in common with the engine under the hood of your car, with one major exception. Like the automotive engine—and the marine diesel and the gasoline stern drive—it is an **internal combustion engine**. That means it burns fuel inside itself to produce power, as opposed to an **external combustion engine**, such as a steam engine, which burns fuel outside itself. The following description applies generally to all internal combustion engines.

The Basic Parts

The basic component of any internal combustion engine is the **engine block**, basically a chunk of metal (in outboards, almost always of aluminum alloy) into which **cylinders** have been drilled. The cylinders may be configured in a single row, in which case the engine is called an **in-line**, or they may be arranged in two rows separated by anywhere from 60 to 90 degrees, in which case the engine is called a **V**. Thus, if both kinds of engines had four cylinders, we would call one an in-line four and the other a V-4.

Inside each cylinder is a **piston**, a slug of metal (usually aluminum alloy) slightly smaller than the cylinder so it can slide up and down. Around its circumference and near its top are grooves (usually three) into which fit resilient metal **piston rings** that press up against the walls of the cylinders creating a tight seal.

Onto the top of this block (or more accurately, onto the top of each bank of cylinders) bolts a cast plate (in outboards, also of aluminum) designed so that when in place it creates a sealed space in each cylinder between itself and the top of the piston. This space is called the

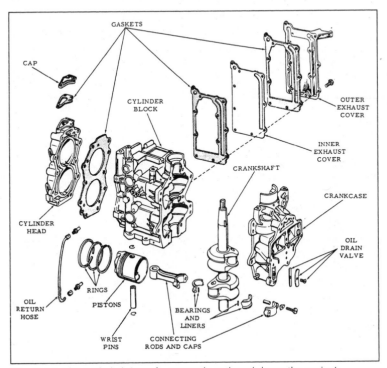

Figure 1-1 This exploded view of a two-cycle outboard shows the engine's principal components. (Courtesy OMC)

combustion chamber and is where the engine burns fuel. Between this plate, called the **cylinder head**, and the block is a resilient metal/fiber **gasket**, which ensures a tight seal. The cylinder head is fastened to the block with bolts.

Although the piston moves up and down the cylinder, it never travels all the way to the top and touches the cylinder head; there is always a small area left between piston and cylinder head.

Compression in a Gasoline Engine

If you were to measure the volume of the combustion chamber when the piston is at the bottom of its travel and compare it with the volume when the piston is at the top of its travel, you would come up with a pair of numbers called the **compression ratio**. For instance, in an engine with a six-to-one (written 6:1) compression ratio, each piston leaves six times more volume when it's at the bottom of its travel than when it's at the top. The size of the compression ratio varies markedly among engine types.

Regardless of whether we're speaking of a fireplace or a boat engine, the object is the same: to produce heat by the burning or combustion of fuel. All combustion requires three things: fuel, oxygen, and air. In your fireplace, that usually means wood, room air, and a match.

To make combustion occur in an internal combustion engine we need to admit fuel—in this case, gasoline—and fresh air into the combustion chamber. Once they are there in the proper proportion we then must supply a heat source to ignite the mixture. In a gasoline engine, the heat source is provided by an electrical arc that jumps between the **poles** or **electrodes** of a **spark plug**.

If you were to place a small amount of gasoline in a bowl in the presence of fresh, oxygenated air and touch a match to it, you'd get combustion. (Take my word; please don't try it.) The gasoline near the surface would burn first and relatively quickly, but that below the surface would take longer because air couldn't get to it. It might not even burn at all if the fresh air in the immediate vicinity were consumed. Still, the process would generate some heat that theoretically could serve to perform some work.

If you took the same amount of gasoline and sprayed it into the air so that each droplet was surrounded by fresh air—in other words, if you **atomized** the gasoline—you'd get much more uniform and complete combustion, and so produce significantly more heat per unit of fuel.

Now imagine spraying a mixture of gasoline and air inside a cylinder when the piston is roughly at the bottom of its travel, then sealing the space, and squeezing the mixture to, say, one-sixth its original volume. This time when you ignited it you'd produce even more heat out of the same fuel, and you'd have done it more quickly and completely.

You would have to be careful because when you compress air you raise its temperature. If compressed too much, a mixture of gasoline and air will ignite all by itself, not from an electrical spark but from the heat generated by compression. The fuel/air mixture could explode while the piston is still traveling upward, causing a collision and a loud bang or knock. If the collision, technically called **detonation**, is severe, it can actually blow a hole right through the top of the piston.

Oil companies put additives in gasoline to make it resist such spontaneous ignition, an ability that is reflected in a gasoline's **octane rating**. But even with high-octane gasoline, 11:1 is about the highest compression ratio possible in a four-cycle engine, and 6.5:1 is about as high as you'll see in a two-cycle outboard engine. High compression ratios may make for more horsepower and better fuel efficiency, but they also generate greater forces that can make an engine run rougher and even tear it apart.

The Rest of the Story

Regardless of whether it comes from gasoline or diesel fuel, the heat produced in an engine's combustion chamber generates **expansion**, forcing the piston down the cylinder. Each piston has a horizontal shaft running through its center onto which clamps the smaller end of a **connecting rod**. The other, larger end of the connecting rod clamps to the arm of a **crankshaft**. Since both ends contain bearings that allow the rod to pivot, the crankshaft translates the vertical motion of the piston into rotary motion that can turn a wheel, generator, pump, or propeller. In multiple-cylinder engines, the crankshaft arms are at different angles, allowing each piston to reach the top of its cylinder at a different time, producing regularly spaced firing and smoother running.

To make any engine last, friction and heat must be controlled. Too much of either will destroy an engine. To control heat, builders cast blocks and cylinder heads with internal passages through which cooling liquid can be circulated via an engine-driven **pump**. In your car, the coolant is routed to the radiator where air passing over its fins dissipates heat. An outboard **cooling system** consists of simply circulating the virtually unlimited supply of relatively cool water in which it is running.

You may think that the more heat you can remove from an engine the better, but this isn't entirely true. Remember that the purpose of the entire internal combustion process is to generate heat that can be put to work. If an engine runs too cold, the walls of the combustion chamber will cool or **quench** the expanding gases, producing incomplete combustion, and less expansion and power.

The final major component of an internal combustion engine is the **lubrication system**. All internal combustion engines rely upon lubricating oil to keep their internal parts from burning up, but the outboard is unique in that, unlike the four-cycle gasoline engine and the diesel, it does not rely on the recirculation of an internal reservoir of oil. Instead, it uses oil that is mixed with gasoline. Precisely how this works is the subject of Chapter 7.

In this chapter we've discussed the basic components of the internal combustion engine and touched on a few of the differences between the principal types of marine engines. In the next chapter, we'll look at how the two- and four-stroke gasoline engines differ. Once again, we'll assume all gasoline-powered stern drives use the **four-stroke cycle** while all outboards use the **two-stroke cycle**.

2

How the Two-Stroke Engine Burns Fuel

Since most outboards use the two-stroke cycle, understanding this system's basic principles of operation is critical to understanding the engine. As the name implies, in the two-stroke cycle (or more commonly, just the "two-stroke") gasoline engine each piston makes two strokes—one up and one down—to generate one **power stroke**. In contrast, your automobile's engine, which uses the four-stroke cycle, requires four piston strokes to generate one stroke of power. While there are variations among two-stroke gasoline engines, all follow the same basic operating principles outlined below.

Before continuing, it's important that you know two critical differences between the two-stroke and the four-stroke. Unlike four-strokes, in which each cylinder has poppet valves in its cylinder head to admit the air-fuel charge and let the exhaust out, two-cycle outboard engines rely solely on holes, or **ports**, cast into the cylinder walls. The movement of the piston up and down the cylinder covers and uncovers these ports, providing the crucial timing needed for proper combustion; there is no mechanical opening and closing of a complex **valve train**. Typically, the **exhaust port** is located slightly above the **intake port**, so it opens sooner and closes later.

The other important difference is the way two-strokes and four-strokes pump air and fuel into the cylinders and pump exhaust out. The four-stroke dedicates one of its four strokes (called the **intake stroke**) to creating a partial vacuum in the cylinder that pulls the intake charge in. It dedicates another full stroke (called the **exhaust stroke**) to pumping exhaust gases out of the cylinder. The distinction is an important one since an engine's power, efficiency, and emissions level are dependent upon how much clean air and fuel gets into the

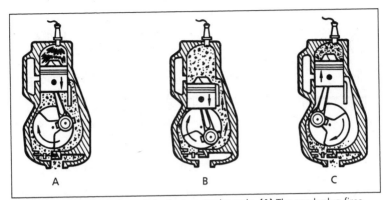

Figure 2-1 The principal events in the two-stroke cycle. **(A)** The spark plug fires, forcing the piston down the cylinder and turning the crankshaft. At the same time the underside of the piston pressurizes the crankcase, forcing the fuel and air up the intake port on the right side. **(B)** The piston passes the exhaust port on the left first, allowing the exhaust to escape, and then passes the intake port on the right, allowing fuel and air to enter the cylinder. **(C)** The piston rises and compresses the fuel and air after closing both ports. At the same time the rising piston creates a partial vacuum in the crankcase, causing more fuel and air to rush past the reed valve. (Courtesy MotorBoat Magazine)

cylinder and how much exhaust and unburned fuel gets out (a process engineers call **scavenging**) during each cycle.

Lacking the two extra strokes, the two-stroke outboard must rely on other devices and procedures to get a charge into the cylinder and exhaust out. One way it gets the charge into the cylinder is to use the underside of the descending piston to push the charge into the cylinder and push the exhaust out of the cylinder. How this works will become clearer once you understand what happens during a **combustion cycle**.

We enter the two-cycle process with the piston at the bottom of the cylinder, having been driven there by the previous power stroke (or by the **starter**). Both intake and exhaust ports are uncovered. As the piston rises, two things happen. First, inside the cylinder the rising piston begins to compress the fuel-air charge that has been brought in by the previous downward stroke. The piston passes the intake port first, sealing it. The exhaust port remains open for a few microseconds, allowing the piston to pump additional exhaust (along with a small portion of the fuel-air charge) out through it. Finally, the piston passes the exhaust port, and the cylinder is sealed. The piston continues to rise, compressing the charge. This completes the **exhaust/compression stroke**.

Meanwhile, beneath the piston is another sealed chamber, the

crankcase, one for each cylinder. Entrance to each chamber is controlled by a one-way **reed valve**. As the piston rises, it creates a partial vacuum inside the crankcase, pulling the fuel-air charge from the carburetor and through the reed valve.

Back above, the piston is near the top of its travel and the spark plug fires. The fuel-air mixture burns and expands, forcing the piston down the cylinder, turning the crankshaft and, eventually, the propeller. As the piston travels downward, it first uncovers the exhaust port, allowing some of the still-expanding gases to escape. Then it uncovers the intake port, and a new charge rushes into the cylinder, forcing out more exhaust gas. This concludes the **power/intake stroke** and one complete combustion cycle.

Simultaneously the downward-driving piston has pressurized the crankcase. The charge cannot escape back through the one-way reed valve, and so it is forced through an internal passage to the intake port, where it rushes into the cylinder.

You can draw a number of conclusions about the two-stroke from this description. First, the two-stroke devotes less time to scavenging and so doesn't do as good a job of it as the four-stroke. As a result, it burns more fuel to produce an equivalent amount of horsepower. It also allows more unburned fuel to escape out the exhaust port than a four-stroke, which means less fuel efficiency and higher hydrocarbon emissions.

You also might guess that due to its less efficient scavenging the two-stroke makes less horsepower, but the opposite is true. If you had a two-stroke and a four-stroke of equal displacement, the two-stroke would create as much as 60 percent more horsepower than the four-stroke because it generates twice as many power strokes per revolution.

Finally a two-stroke is lighter and smaller than a four-stroke, partially because its main components are aluminum and partially because it doesn't need a complicated valve train; it has no poppet valves, valve springs, rocker arms, push rods, valve lifters, or camshaft. As we'll soon see, it's also lighter because it doesn't need the four-stroke's complicated lubrication system.

Loop-charged Versus Cross-charged

Although the description above applies in general to all two-stroke outboards, there are design variations. The most significant is the path by which the fuel-air charge enters the cylinder. Two designs are common: **loop charging** and **cross charging**. Most domestic outboards rated under 120 h.p. and manufactured before 1986 are cross-charged; higher horsepower and newer domestic models and most Japanese models are loop-charged.

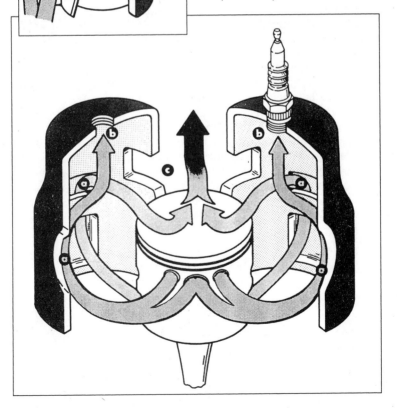

Figure 2-2 A cross-charged engine. Note the side-to-side movement of the gasses **(a)** and the large deflector on the piston **(b)**, which directs the gasses toward the top of the cylinder **(c)**. As the gasses continue to fill the cylinder, they force the burned gasses from the previous power stroke out the exhaust ports **(d)**.

Figure 2-3 An exaggerated drawing of a loop-charged engine's combustion chamber. Note the flat piston and the loop of ports. The arrows depict a complete flow cycle.

Two design features distinguish a loop-charged engine from a cross-charged engine. Both are internal features so it's virtually impossible to tell one kind of engine from another without tearing it apart. The first characteristic is the deployment of the ports. As the name implies, in a loop-charged engine both intake and exhaust ports are arrayed around the circumference of the cylinder wall. This contrasts with the cross-charged engine where the intake and exhaust ports each typically occupy only the opposing sides of the cylinder.

The second design characteristic is a result of the port arrangement. In a cross-charged engine, the piston has an exaggerated **crown**, or **deflector**, on top to route the incoming charge upward toward the spark plug and prevent it from going directly out the exhaust port. This minimizes the loss of charge and improves combustion efficiency. By comparison, a loop-charged engine has a basically flat crown, similar to that of a four-cycle engine.

As you can imagine, a circular array of ports results in both better dispersal of the incoming charge and more complete displacement of the exhaust from the cylinder, meaning superior scavenging. Not surprising, a loop-charged engine is more fuel-efficient, but the advantage is not the same at all engine ratings, nor is it the same at all operating speeds. The efficiency of most loop-charged engines is roughly equivalent to that of cross-charged engines at slow speeds, but the "looper" becomes more fuel-efficient as engine speed increases until, at full throttle, the advantage can be as great as 20 percent.

While loop-charging enjoys an efficiency advantage, it doesn't come free. Cross-charged engines typically run smoother at idle and slow speeds, although the difference can be minimized by altering cylinder and crankshaft configurations and changing engine mounts. Loop-charged engines are also usually more expensive to manufacture, since their port arrangement demands intricate casting for internal passages. For the same reasons, loop-charged engines are also usually heavier. Thus many small-horsepower engines are still cross-charged.

3

The Fuel System

Until the advent of stringent pollution controls in the '80s, the two-cycle outboard engine had one major design feature in common with the familiar four-cycle automotive engine: the **carburetor**. Since the latest round of pollution-control regulations, automotive engineers have devised fuel systems that can make continuous, minute, and precise adjustments in the fuel-to-air ratio, as factors such as load, temperature, and even atmospheric pressure changed. First they fit engines with electronically controlled carburetors, then single-point fuel injection, and finally multiple-point fuel injection. Each step required small but sophisticated microcomputers that could draw engine operating data from a network of sensors.

Someday when such regulations extend to pleasure boats, the outboard engine will be equipped with a similarly sophisticated fuel system. For now, however, all but a few engines from Mercury, Mariner, and Suzuki rely on that simplest, cheapest, and time-proven device, the carburetor, to properly mix fuel and air into a volatile, easily ignitable mixture. Here's how the carburetor and fuel system work on a typical outboard.

The Fuel Pump

Fuel is pulled from the **fuel tank** by a **fuel pump**, just as it is on your automobile. Your car's fuel pump, however, is mechanically driven, where that on the outboard is powered by pressure pulses generated as the piston moves up and down in the crankcase. A **diaphragm** inside the pump separates the crankcase side from the pump side. When pressure spikes in the crankcase, the diaphragm is distended, reducing the volume and increasing pressure on the pump side. When pressure in the crankcase decreases, the opposite occurs.

It is this recurring pressure rise and fall that provides the pumping action. The advantages of the outboard system are reduced size and weight, simplicity, and the need for little horsepower to operate. It's relatively rare for an outboard fuel pump to fail.

On the down side, outboard fuel pumps are small and lack sufficient power to pull fuel all the way from the main fuel tank. They must be **primed**—that is, fuel must initially be brought to them before they'll work. To do this, nearly all outboards rely upon a simple **squeeze bulb** located in the **fuel line** just upstream of the engine. It works essentially the same way as the fuel pump itself: by expansion and contraction. The only difference is that the squeeze bulb relies on your hand for power, while the fuel pump uses crankcase pressure.

After leaving the squeeze bulb, the fuel may or may not pass through a small, cleanable **filter**. (There may also be a large oil-filter-type canister fuel filter upstream of the bulb.) This feature is typically found on newer outboards. Once fuel leaves this filter (if present), it reaches the carburetor or carburetors. If there are multiple carburetors, the fuel line will connect to a **manifold** from which it divides into enough lines to serve each carburetor. As we'll see in a moment, the number of carburetors is dependent upon the number and configuration of the cylinders.

Whether it's on a boat, a car, or a lawn mower, a carburetor must do two things: effectively mix fuel and air into an atomized, easily ignitable mixture in the correct proportions; and adjust the volume of fuel-air mixture admitted to the cylinders to control engine speed and power. It also must periodically modify the fuel-air ratio (or mixture) by adding more fuel (**enriching** the mixture) to provide easier cold starting.

The mixture of fuel and air in just the right proportions takes place in the **venturi** or barrel. Outboard carburetors may have one or two barrels, each of which serves a single cylinder. Single-cylinder and in-line engines of two, three, or four cylinders typically use one single-barrel carburetor per cylinder. V engines usually use one two-barrel carburetor for each pair of opposing cylinders, each of the side-by-side barrels serving one cylinder.

The venturi is simply a carefully sized restriction in the carburetor through which air that is being sucked into the engine must pass. As the air passes through this restriction its velocity increases, lowering the ambient pressure in the venturi.

A machined passage or **jet**, also of a specific size, leads from a small fuel reservoir in the carburetor, called the **carburetor bowl**, into the venturi. The low pressure in the venturi sucks an exact amount of

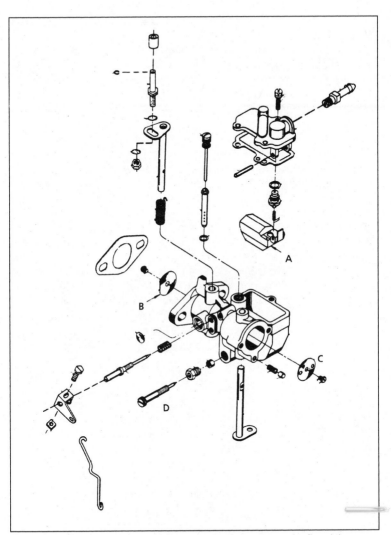

Figure 3-1 An exploded view of an outboard carburetor. Note the float (A), throttle plate (B), choke plate (C), and the adjustable mixture screw (D). (Courtesy OMC)

gasoline through the jet and into the venturi where it hits the high-speed air and disperses into a vapor. The greater the speed of the air moving through the venturi, the more fuel that is drawn from the carburetor bowl. Adjustable **needle valves** can modify the ratio of fuel to air within small limits, and many outboards have individual jets for low and high speed. A simple **float valve** in the carburetor bowl keeps it full of fuel.

The volume of air that passes through the venturi controls the volume of fuel admitted; the volume of the resulting fuel-air charge controls the power output of the engine. The volume of air entering the venturi (and by extension, the amount of fuel) is in turn controlled by a simple **flapper** or **butterfly valve** in the intake air passage downstream of the venturi. When you put your foot on the accelerator in your car or push the throttle lever forward in your boat, you twist the butterfly valve open, allowing more air (and therefore more fuel) to enter the engine. When you reduce speed, the valve closes, restricting both air and fuel, and reducing power.

The Choke

When an engine is cold, proper combustion demands a higher proportion of gasoline in the charge than when it's warm. To effect this, a second flapper valve called the **choke plate** is located upstream of the venturi. The choke plate on most outboards is activated either by pulling a lever or button on the engine or control, or in some cases by depressing the ignition key, which activates a **solenoid**. As soon as the engine starts, the choke can be opened, either partially or completely.

Some newer outboards eliminate the choke plate altogether, replacing it with a solenoid-operated system that squirts a shot of raw gasoline into each carburetor throat at the time of cold start. Since this also enriches the mixture, it has the same effect as a conventional choke.

There is one more carburetor component in our simple carburetor worth discussing. Because it takes a moment for the flow of fuel to adjust to the increased flow of air when the throttle is suddenly opened, there can be an annoying lag between throttle movement and engine reaction. To avoid this, some carburetors have a device called an **accelerator pump**, which pulls a shot of gasoline from the carburetor bowl and injects it directly into the venturi when the throttle is suddenly opened. This allows the engine to respond more quickly.

The Ignition System

If the outboard gasoline engine has a weak link it is the ignition system. The reason is simple: High voltage and a damp environment don't mix. Add a little salt, which increases both the rate of corrosion and the conductivity of water, and you have the potential for serious problems. For all these reasons, it's important to understand how your outboard's ignition system works and how to take care of it. If you have an engine problem, chances are it will occur in its electrical/ignition system.

Fortunately ignition system design and maintenance are simple. In keeping with the philosophy of this book, our explanation of the ignition system also will be simplistic and devoid of electrical theory.

The outboard ignition system differs from that on automobiles—and it's simpler. Differences aside, both systems have two primary functions. One is to boost **12-volt battery** or **alternator current** to between 20,000 and 40,000 volts, so it can jump the 0.035-inch air gap between a spark plug's electrodes. The other is to make sure the spark plug fires at precisely the right time.

There are three basic types of outboard ignition systems: **flywheel magneto** with **breaker points**, flywheel magneto without breaker points (also called **solid-state ignition**), and **capacitor discharge**. All are located up under the flywheel out of sight. Most newer outboards use either breakerless magneto or capacitive discharge ignition (CDI) because they are virtually maintenance-free. Moreover, CDI systems can produce up to 40,000 volts at the spark plug, which means less chance of spark plugs fouling and misfiring. By contrast, breaker-point systems are typically limited to about 20,000 volts, and the points must be periodically adjusted and replaced along with the condenser.

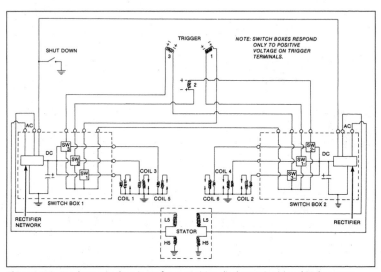

Figure 4-1 A schematic drawing of a capacitive discharge ignition (CDI) system for a V-6 outboard. Note the six coils in the center of the diagram, one for each cylinder.

The precise way each of these systems works is beyond the scope of this book, but since most modern outboards use CDI, we'll give you a brief sketch of that system. Up under the flywheel is the mechanism for timing and distributing the low-voltage electrical impulses, and at each spark plug there is an ignition coil that jumps the voltage to as much as 40,000 volts. Because of this design, one or more coils (depending upon the number of cylinders in the engine) can fail, yet the engine still can run. This compares to the automotive engine in which if the single coil fails the engine will not run.

Distribution

The coil may successfully jump voltage from 12 to 40,000 volts, but the engine *must* have some mechanism to get the current *to* each coil and spark plug at precisely the correct time or the engine will not run. As with everything else about the two-cycle engine, the system for doing this is remarkably simple.

Under the toothed flywheel on top of the engine is a series of **stationary electromagnets** (small coils of wire connected to the ignition), and another **permanent magnet** attached to the crankshaft. Basically each time the moving permanent magnet passes a stationary electromagnet, it sends a charge to a particular coil, which then increases the voltage and sends it on to the spark plug.

The order in which the cylinders fire is theoretically determined by the order of the stationary magnets. In practice an engine usually will only run properly with a specific firing order.

Exactly when the spark plugs fire is called **ignition timing**. It's regulated by the position of the group of magnets relative to the moving magnet. Rotating the plate on which the electromagnets are mounted in one direction makes the spark plugs fire sooner relative to the pistons' position in their cylinders. Rotating it the other way makes the spark plugs fire later.

That's important, because at slow speeds the spark plugs fire just before the piston reaches the top of the cylinder, so that by the time the fuel actually burns, the piston is in position to be forced down. As engine speed increases, the time necessary for the fuel to ignite remains the same but the piston moves faster, so the spark plug must fire a little earlier to "lead" the piston. This is called **ignition advance**. The outboard ignition advance employs a simple mechanical linkage between the plate holding the magnets and the throttle so that as the throttle is advanced, the ignition automatically advances, and as the throttle is closed, the ignition retards.

As you can imagine, wires leading from the coils to the spark plugs must be well insulated, otherwise the 40,000-volt current will jump to some other component, such as the engine block, which is "ground" in this electrical circuit, and the spark plug will fail to fire. Spark plug wires can wear out after many hours, but the most likely source of trouble is where the wire connects to the spark plug. Here, the contact may loosen from being pulled off and pushed on too many times, or its protective **rubber boot** may become brittle and cracked with age, allowing moisture or oil to enter. Again, the result is a short circuit and a misfire.

Spark Plugs

Spark plugs are relatively simple devices designed to make sure that high-voltage current stays isolated from the surrounding cylinder head so that a strong spark will jump the gap between spark plug tip and spark plug electrode and ignite the fuel/air mixture.

There are three things to remember about spark plugs. First, choose the right one. A spark plug must fit into the threaded hole in the cylinder head and not protrude too far into the cylinder. It also must have the proper heat range—a measure of its ability to dissipate heat produced by combustion. A spark plug that is too hot wears out quickly; one too cold becomes fouled by unburned fuel and fails to fire. Choose the spark plug recommended by your engine builder and you should have no problem with heat range unless you operate under unusual conditions.

The second consideration is proper installation. Spark plugs are not

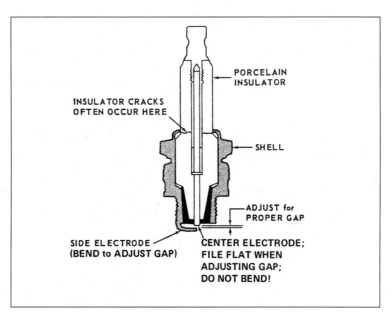

Figure 4-2 A cutaway view of a typical spark plug. (Courtesy Mercury Marine)

properly gapped when you buy them. Before you install a spark plug, you must adjust the gap between the tip and electrode. For this job you'll need the recommended spark plug gap from your owner's manual and an inexpensive **feeler gauge** with a small notched tool to bend the electrode. It shouldn't need much force; in many cases a light tap will do the trick. Use a light touch or you may put the electrode out of alignment with the tip.

When screwed into the cylinder head, the spark plug also must be tightened enough to prevent leaks, yet not be tightened so much that its fragile ceramic insulator is damaged. Most mechanics can feel when they've cranked a plug down hard enough to collapse its brass gasket and get a good seal without causing damage. If you haven't developed such a feel, rent a **torque wrench**, which will tell you exactly how tight you're twisting the plugs. You should find spark plug torque specifications in your owner's manual, but if you can't locate them, 14 pound-feet is usually a safe number.

Finally maintain your plugs. Thanks to unleaded gasoline, spark plugs enjoy a long life today. Although many boat owners prefer to replace plugs each year, most plugs should last at least 300 hours before replacement, which for most people works out to two to three boating seasons. However, there is no arguing that a fresh set of plugs every spring is cheap insurance.

Above all, remember this about the ignition system: It is designed to provide a spark of sufficient strength to jump an air gap of 0.035 inch. This ability not only ensures your engine will run efficiently, it also means the current can jump other gaps. High-voltage current will always take the path of least resistance, which might mean a hairline crack in a spark plug insulator, a dirty spark plug boot, or even a piece of frayed or worn spark plug wire.

Keep all the high- and low-voltage components of your engine clean and in proper condition. By doing so you'll vastly reduce the chances of ignition problems—and that means fewer engine problems overall.

The Cooling System

Regardless of the number of strokes in its cycle or where it is installed, the internal combustion engine is designed first to produce heat, then put it to work. The amount of heat it produces must be restricted to a relatively narrow range. Too little means the engine is inefficient and makes too little power; too much means damage to, or even destruction of, the engine. It is the job of the **cooling system** to ensure that an engine strikes just the right balance between the two extremes.

The basic principle of most engine cooling systems is **heat exchange**; that is, transferring excess heat of combustion to some other medium and away from the engine. In your car, heat exchange is effected by a recirculating supply of coolant that surrounds the block and removes heat from it, then travels to the radiator where it transfers this heat through the walls of the radiator and into the surrounding air that passes over it. Consequently, the automotive radiator is termed a water-to-air heat exchanger.

Instead of transferring engine heat to water and then to air, the outboard's cooling system transfers it directly to the virtually unlimited supply of relatively cool water in which it operates. It does this using an engine-driven **water pump** to pull water from an intake on the bottom of the **lower unit**, circulate it through all **internal powerhead cavities**, and then pump it back out. In most outboards this pump is mounted inside the **intermediate unit**, just above the large, flat **anti-cavitation plate**. Some of the cooling water may also exit through a bypass on the intermediate unit just above the water line, where there is less back pressure at slow speed, and out a small **pee hole** that serves as a telltale to let you know the engine is pumping water.

The main advantages of a raw-water cooling system are simplicity and low cost. Other than the water pump, the only other component of note is a **thermostat** for each cylinder bank. This thermostat restricts coolant flow to speed warm-up and help the engine maintain a minimum temperature.

The amount of durability and maintenance required by a raw-water cooling system depends upon the quality of the water in which it operates. Such a system can offer years of trouble-free service in freshwater lakes and rivers with little or no attention. In salt or polluted water, however, the result of ignored maintenance can be corrosion and the build-up of **scale** and deposits in internal passages. Scale inhibits the transfer of heat and can restrict the passage of cooling water, eventually leading to overheating.

The raw-water pump's **impeller** is made of rubber or synthetic rubber-like material. Under normal conditions it will last many years, but two conditions can render it useless in short order. One is running it dry. Not only does the pump push water around the block, it uses that water as a lubricant and coolant. Without water, the pump's impeller vanes heat up from friction and melt or deform.

The other problem is ingestion of sand or grit. If you operate your outboard while the unit is near the bottom where the propeller will stir up sand, the raw-water impeller will suck in sand, which will act as an abrasive, quickly wearing out the rubber impeller blades. The solution here is to not run your outboard unless the water intake is submerged, and to keep it well off a sandy bottom.

Some boat owners prefer to change the water pump impeller each season as a preventive measure. Others simply wait for it to wear out (as evidenced by a weak stream from the pee hole), something that can take many years. Whichever course you select, changing an impeller is a job you can do if you're prepared. To reach it you must drain the lower unit lube oil, then remove the lower unit from the intermediate unit by unscrewing the bolts on the bottom side of the anti-cavitation plate. This exposes the pump, whose impeller usually can be pulled out by hand or with pliers.

Inserting the new impeller is often easier if you wet it or coat it with light oil or petroleum jelly, then twist it into place, making sure you twist in the same direction it normally runs. Replace the lower unit gasket, bolt on the lower unit, refill the oil, and touch up any chipped paint. Before you head out, test the engine in water to make sure everything's OK. After you've done this once or twice, you may want to keep an impeller and gasket in your spare parts kit for emergencies.

The Exhaust System

Like the exhaust system in your automobile's engine, the one in your outboard is designed to route toxic exhaust gases safely out of the engine and into the atmosphere in such a way that they won't be inhaled by passengers. Both systems are also designed to reduce the sound produced by combustion, although the outboard engine silences exhaust differently than does a car or truck engine. Today most automotive exhaust systems have a muffler to reduce exhaust sound and a catalytic converter to reduce the level of pollutants in the exhaust gases. Boats have yet to adopt this latter technology, although that may change when environmental regulations become more strict.

The outboard accomplishes these tasks by using the resource it has most of: water. All cylinders in an outboard engine are configured so that they dump their exhaust into a common **manifold**. On in-line engines this is usually identifiable as a large box-like structure on the side of the engine, all the way aft. On V engines, it's the large area at the very back between the two cylinder banks.

Once exhaust enters this chamber, it encounters water that already has been circulated around the engine to cool it. The warm water mixes with the hot exhaust gases, lowering their temperature. This not only keeps things safe beneath the engine cowling, it also lowers the **acoustical energy** of the gases. Acoustical energy, which is what makes the exhaust gases produce noise, is partly related to heat. As a result when the gas temperature drops, so does the noise level.

After leaving the manifold, the exhaust/water mixture passes down through a separate passage in the drive unit. Just beneath the powerhead there is usually an opening or **relief port** where some of the gases and water can escape. Those which do not exit this **exhaust bypass**

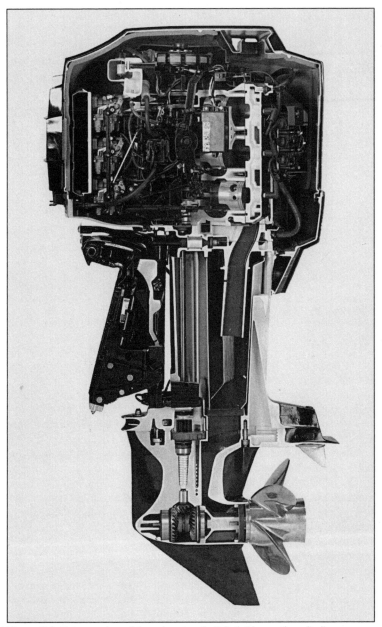

Figure 6-1 Cutaway view of the exhaust path. Exhaust leaves the cylinders, passes through the lower unit, and exits through the propeller. (Courtesy Mercury Marine)

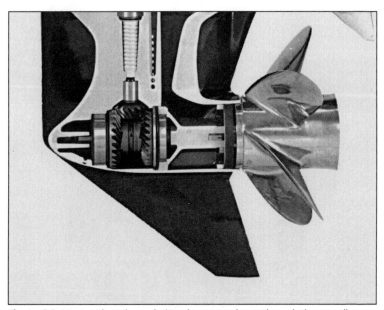

Figure 6-2 Most outboards are designed to pass exhaust through the propeller, which reduces back pressure when the boat is underway. (Courtesy Mercury Marine)

travel farther down the drive unit and eventually exit via a passage that takes them through the middle of the lower unit and propeller, and into the low-pressure water immediately behind the moving propeller. (On some smaller outboards with propellers too small to accommodate this exhaust passage, exhaust instead exits through a passage on the bottom of the anti-ventilation plate.)

The exhaust bypass is critical to proper engine performance because at slow speeds the water behind the propeller doesn't move much and restricts the ability of the exhaust gases to escape. This **back pressure** normally would prevent the engine from running properly at slow speeds, but the exhaust bypass gives it a place to escape. However, if a boat is so heavily loaded that this passage becomes submerged, the bypass cannot do its job and engine damage may result.

Unlike the exhaust systems of the stern drive and inboard, the outboard's is virtually maintenance-free. Since almost all components are of aluminum alloy, corrosion is not of great concern. However, there is often a large sacrificial zinc immediately in front of the propeller that should be checked once each year. You normally have to pull the propeller off to get to it.

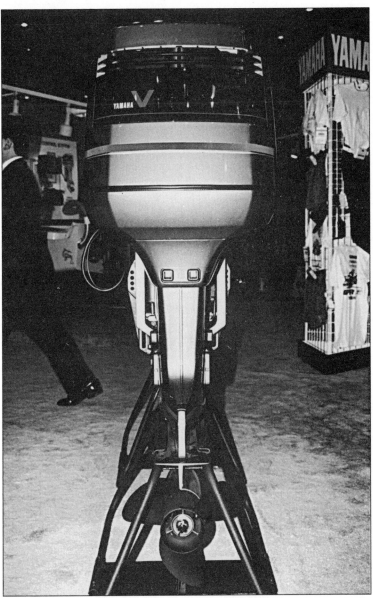

Figure 6-3 The center section of the propeller through which the exhaust passes is easily seen on the rear of this Yamaha outboard. The two square ports about halfway up are bypass ports through which exhaust passes when the engine idles. (Courtesy Yamaha)

The Lubrication System

Rub two solids together and you get heat. Rub them together fast enough and you'll get a lot of heat—maybe even fire. Rub them together long enough and you'll not only get heat, you'll eventually wear them away. But separate the solids with a minuscule film of something slippery—like oil—and you'll vastly reduce both heat and wear. In other words, you'll reduce friction.

That is the simple principle behind all lubrication, including that which takes place in an engine. In your car, an internal engine-driven pump constantly recirculates oil to all critical moving parts. The two-cycle's system of lubrication is different and—you guessed it—simpler.

In a two-cycle outboard motor there is no reservoir of oil and no engine-driven recirculating oil pump. So how does oil get into the engine and work its way to all the necessary parts? By combining with gasoline. This may be done manually, by pouring the proper amount of oil into the fuel tank at fill up, or by mechanically adding oil as needed from an external reservoir. In either case, the principle of lubrication is the same.

As we described in Chapter 3, fuel enters the engine at the carburetor where it mixes with air. It then passes into the crankcase through a one-way reed valve so it cannot escape when the crankcase is pressurized by the descending piston. At any point in this process—at the fuel line going into the carburetor, just after the carburetor, or inside the crankcase—oil may be mechanically injected; exactly where depends upon the particular system design.

Once the fuel-oil mixture enters the hot crankcase, the oil "flashes off"; that is, it separates from the gasoline, turns into a mist, and covers

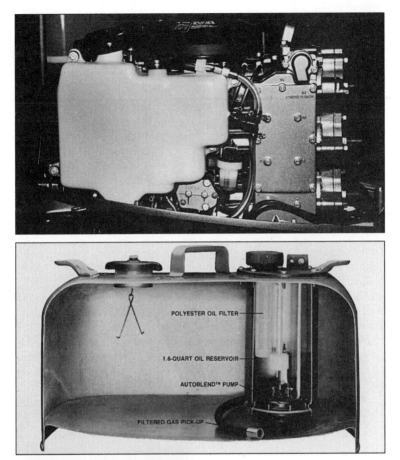

Figure 7-1 Usually boaters must mix oil with the gasoline in the outboard's fuel tank, but there are alternative systems available. This Yamaha outboard features automatic oil injection. Note the oil tank mounted on the engine. OMC's Autoblend R, left, automatically adds oil to the fuel line at a constant 100:1 ratio. Autoblend, above, mixes oil and gasoline inside a portable six-gallon tank.

all the moving parts in the crankcase. (Since the two-cycle engine has no valve train, virtually all of the engine's moving parts are in the crankcase or accessible from it.) The remaining lighter gasoline continues on out of the crankcase, into the intake port, and eventually into the combustion chamber.

Like other features of the two-cycle engine, this lubrication system emphasizes simplicity, but at a cost. First, when enough oil accumulates in the crankcase it passes into the combustion chamber where it burns along with gasoline. Since oil, like gasoline, is a hydrocarbon, it too can function as fuel. Since it doesn't burn as completely as gasoline, it produces blue smoke that passes out the exhaust. In older engines unburned oil in the combustion chamber also can coat the spark plugs and foul them, causing misfiring. Finally, if the crankcase is cold, such as during initial start-up, the oil doesn't initially flash off completely, resulting in more smoke.

To some degree, these problems have been ameliorated—although not eliminated—by **automatic oiling systems**, which may vary the ratio of gasoline and oil according to engine speed. Depending on design, they may add one part of oil for every 150 or even 200 parts of gasoline while the engine is at idle, then increase it to a 1:50 ratio at high speed. By contrast, manually mixed gasoline and oil (often called **pre-mix**) is measured at a constant ratio of 50 parts of gasoline to one of oil, and the engine must burn that oil no matter what its speed, even though it doesn't need all of it at slower speeds. Of course, automatic oiling systems aren't perfect; they add both complexity and cost to an engine.

The Propulsion System

The outboard propulsion system performs two primary duties. It attaches to the powerhead crankshaft and transmits power down a vertical shaft and through a 90-degree gear set. Thus, power transmitted by a vertical engine shaft can turn a propeller on a horizontal shaft a couple of feet below. This design takes maximum advantage of the compact design of the two-cycle engine, and allows the entire engine/propulsion package to hang on the transom instead of taking up space inside the boat.

Like the stern drive, the outboard is an **articulated power system**, meaning its propeller can move from side to side for steering and pivot up and down for trimming and tilting. The former ability eliminates the need for a separate rudder and steering gear. It also provides better maneuverability and steering response, since the direction of propeller thrust changes when the wheel is turned. The latter ability means a driver can change the boat's **running attitude** (how high or low its bow is) to suit water and operating conditions, or **tilt** it up far enough so it can be beached or trailered without damaging the engine or propeller.

Most outboards also incorporate internal mechanisms for changing the direction of propeller rotation in the same way that the transmission does in an automobile, offering forward, reverse, or neutral. This eliminates the need for a separate, external transmission and, therefore, reduces the size of the package while enhancing the flexibility and maneuverability of the boat.

What follows is a basic explanation of how the outboard propulsion system works. Although there are a number of minor variations on this basic theme, the principles and operational procedures are largely identical. That's what you need to know.

The Path of Power

Outboards consist of three main parts; the **powerhead** or engine, the **intermediate housing**, and the **lower unit**. Steering is effected by pivoting the entire assembly on a fourth component, the **transom bracket**. The entire assembly can pivot vertically on this bracket usually via **hydraulic rams** and the pump that powers these cylinders is electrically operated.

A vertical shaft attaches to the vertical powerhead crankshaft, passes down through the intermediate housing, and terminates in the lower unit. About midway down, this shaft has a toothed portion that drives the **raw-water pump**. The shaft terminates in a **pinion gear** that allows a 90-degree change of direction so the output or propeller shaft can be roughly horizontal.

At this point, the propeller shaft is permanently engaged with the

Figure 8-1 This exploded view shows all the major components of the outboard drive train including the clutch dog, drive shaft, and propeller shaft. The assembly in the upper right is the water pump. (Courtesy Mercury Marine)

engine, so some sort of mechanism is necessary to disengage it and shift it from forward to reverse. The solution is the same mechanism used in some stern drives: the **dog clutch**. Indeed, the lower unit of these stern drives is virtually identical to and actually derived from that of the outboard.

The pinion gear on the end of the vertical shaft constantly meshes with two horizontal pinion gears, one forward of it and the other to the rear. This placement means that one gear constantly turns clockwise while the other constantly turns counter-clockwise.

The Dog Clutch

On the inside face of each of these horizontal pinions is a **dog**, basically a circular piece of metal with square protrusions and matching indentations, so that it looks like the top of a castle wall. Between these two counter-rotating gear-dog sets is a **double-dog piece**, with an identical castellated surface facing each of the counter-rotating dogs. This piece attaches to but slides horizontally along the propeller shaft, so it always turns with it.

When the double-dog set is exactly in the middle, it engages neither the front nor rear dog, providing neutral. When you move the throttle/ shift lever in one direction, the double-dog set slides forward, clunks into place, and the propeller turns in one direction. When you move the throttle/control in the opposite direction, the center dog set moves out of engagement with the forward dog, through the middle where there is no engagement, and clunks into engagement with the rear dog, providing the opposite propeller rotation.

As you can see, the main advantage of the dog clutch is its durability and simplicity; it's been proved in decades of use and there are relatively few moving parts. Its principal disadvantages are the clunk when the dogs engage and the limits on the amount of **torque** (or twisting force) it can handle.

To make engagement and disengagement smoother and easier, the sides of the dogs are slightly inclined. These ramps allow the dogs to engage and disengage more easily. However, if sufficient torque is applied, the dogs can pop out of engagement on their own. Fortunately for outboard owners, it takes a large, powerful engine to make this happen, usually a 7.4-liter or larger four-cycle V-8. In engines of smaller displacement or two-cycle engines, accidental disengagement rarely if ever occurs.

Many boaters with twin-engine boats prefer to have their propellers turn in opposite directions because they feel that counter-rotating propellers make the boat track straighter. To do this in an outboard, one unit must be built differently than the other, a factor which makes this preference a more expensive option.

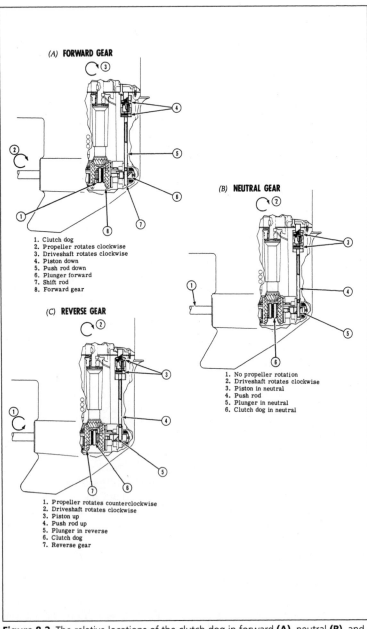

(A) FORWARD GEAR

1. Clutch dog
2. Propeller rotates clockwise
3. Driveshaft rotates clockwise
4. Piston down
5. Push rod down
6. Plunger forward
7. Shift rod
8. Forward gear

(B) NEUTRAL GEAR

1. No propeller rotation
2. Driveshaft rotates clockwise
3. Piston in neutral
4. Push rod
5. Plunger in neutral
6. Clutch dog in neutral

(C) REVERSE GEAR

1. Propeller rotates counterclockwise
2. Driveshaft rotates clockwise
3. Piston up
4. Push rod up
5. Plunger in reverse
6. Clutch dog
7. Reverse gear

Figure 8-2 The relative locations of the clutch dog in forward **(A)**, neutral **(B)**, and reverse **(C)**. (Courtesy OMC)

Trim and Tilt

Nearly all outboards can pivot forward and back. Smaller ones must be moved physically, then set mechanically into position, but most outboards of 25 h.p. and larger can be ordered with electric trim and tilt, meaning their position can be altered electrically while the boat is underway. This allows a boater to point propeller thrust slightly downward to keep the bow down and put the boat onto plane faster while maintaining better visibility. Or by aiming propeller thrust slightly upward he or she can raise the bow once the boat is on plane to reduce the amount of hull touching the water, thereby improving performance and efficiency. Furthermore, by extending the drive even farther out and up—by tilting it—the boater can operate the boat in very shallow water or put it on a trailer or beach without dragging the engine and prop.

To do this, the outboard has either one or two **hydraulic cylinders** attached to its transom bracket, activated by an electrical pump mounted on the bracket. When the boater pushes a button on the control or instrument panel, these cylinders are activated in unison; the direction in which they move is determined by the direction in which the button is pushed. To activate the tilt mode and swing the drive all the way up, it's usually necessary to hold the button down longer, or sometimes to push another button altogether.

Another feature of the outboard trim system, whether mechanical or electrical, is **kick-up**. Most outboards have a lever on the bracket or a bypass valve in the hydraulic cylinders that allows the entire unit to swing up out of the way almost instantly when it hits an object, preventing damage to the lower unit. The thrust of the propeller eventually forces the drive back into position.

If you look at the typical outboard intermediate housing you can see that there's a lot of space for things other than the drive shaft, gears, and clutches. Indeed, the unit also contains passages for cooling water to be drawn through and supplied to the engine, or to be exhausted back into the water, and for exhaust to pass through and out via the propeller. Moreover, gear sets typically run in a special oil that must be periodically changed, so reservoirs for the oil must also be included.

Obviously, it's imperative that lube oil, raw water, and exhaust be segregated from each other, and this is done with gaskets and seals.

Two more components worth mentioning that are found on all outboards are the **anti-ventilation plate** (sometimes called the **anti-cavitation plate**) and the **trim tab**. The anti-cavitation plate is the wide, flat plate just above the propeller that runs from the front of the drive to the rear. It has two functions: to provide lift and help in planing, and to prevent the propeller from sucking air from the surface, or ventilat-

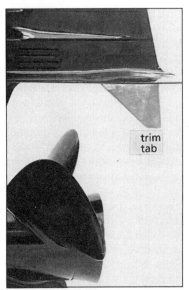

Figure 8-3 The trim tab is located on the underside of the anti-ventilation plate. The tab can pivot to either side. (Courtesy Mercury Marine)

ing. Ventilation occurs when the drive unit is trimmed too far out, and as a result the propeller loses its bite, the engine speeds up, and the boat slows down. In most cases, the remedy is simply to trim the drive unit down far enough to allow the propeller to bite again.

The other component is a small fin on the underside of the anti-ventilation plate immediately above the propeller; this is called the trim tab. Its job is to help offset steering feedback or torque produced by the rotating propeller. Without it, the boat's wheel usually pulls in one direction, which can quickly tire the driver and in extreme cases be dangerous. Once you loosen the bolt that holds the trim tab you can rotate the tab in the opposite

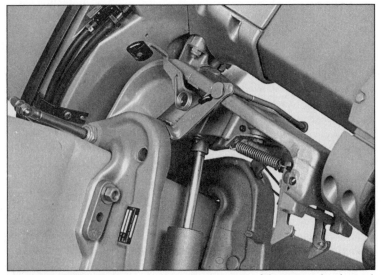

Figure 8-4 A trim cylinder may be located in the center of the transom bracket and connected to the lower unit. (Courtesy OMC)

direction of the torque, just like a boat rudder. When the tab is properly adjusted and the boat is properly trimmed, you should be able to take your hands off the wheel and the boat should follow a relatively straight course.

Anti-Corrosion Measures

Because so much of the outboard is immersed in water so much of its life, corrosion can be a problem. To understand how an outboard corrodes and how you can prevent it you need to understand how corrosion works. The most common kind of corrosion in the marine environment is **electrolysis**, which occurs when two dissimilar metals are immersed in water that contains sufficient impurities to allow the water to conduct an electrical current. (This is the same principle by which the typical automotive battery works.) Electrons from one metal (the less **noble**, or stable, one) travel to the other (the more noble one) until the less noble metal eventually dissolves.

The outboard's intermediate and lower unit housings are cast of aluminum alloy containing small amounts of other metals added to make it strong and easy to work. If you place this alloy into salt, brackish, or polluted water and there is another, less reactive metal in the same water, the aluminum will dissolve.

Outboards are protected from such corrosion four ways. First, they are cast from the most corrosion-resistant alloys available. Each company formulates its own unique alloy, which it thinks offers the best mix of strength and corrosion resistance. Second, every component that comes into contact with the water is painted with the hardest, most durable paint available, because if the water can't reach the metal, it can't react with it. Again, each company has its own unique way of preparing, priming, and painting the castings, as well as its own unique paint formula.

Third, the outboard is equipped with a number of exposed, unpainted zinc components because zinc is the metal most susceptible to electrolytic corrosion. These inexpensive, easily replaceable, sacrificial zincs dissolve first, saving more costly components. Typical zinc locations are inside the lower unit forward of the propeller, on the underside of the transom bracket, and on the upper portion of the lower unit. Mercury, for example, makes its trim tab out of zinc, so that as it wears away you are warned by an increase in steering torque. Because they are never painted (and never should be) and are in clear view (except for the one ahead of the propeller), zincs are easy to spot. Just look for pieces of silver metal.

As one final step in protecting outboards, builders make sure everything that might be exposed to water is electrically connected or

bonded to each other. A component not bonded is not protected by the zincs and will begin to corrode.

In addition to these anti-corrosion measures, Mercury offers an electronic device that stops electrolytic corrosion by imparting a tiny blocking current to the water around the drive. Called MerCathode, it's compatible with other types of outboards and draws little current from the battery. However, if the outboard can be tilted completely clear of the water, such a unit is usually unnecessary.

 **PART TWO**

How to Operate Your Outboard

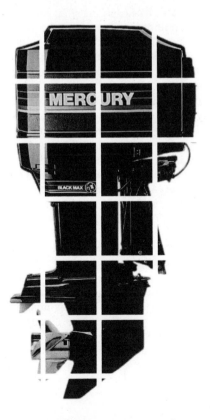

The Log

Boating is fun, but it also has a serious side. Part of that side is taking care of your boat and outboard motor so that they will give you years of trouble-free operation. Although extremely reliable and durable, the outboard is neither perfect nor immune to wear and tear. But if you operate it wisely and care for it properly, it can last as long as the hull to which it is mounted.

The key to maintaining an outboard, or any mechanical device for that matter, is **systematic maintenance**. And the key to systematic maintenance is keeping good records. No one can predict a catastrophic breakdown, but fortunately, most mechanical problems do not just pop up out of the blue. An engine or drive unit usually gives fair warning that something is wrong well before it quits. Your job is to know these signs, observe them, and take the proper action when you see them. Your single most valuable tool in observing long-term trends is a log, a simple written record of what you observe and what you and others do to your boat and outboard.

In the following two chapters you'll find two checklists; one you should refer to every time you take your boat out, no matter how short the trip. The other is a more involved checklist, which you should refer to every month. Each time you conduct either check, write the results in your **log**. Your log need be nothing more than a pocket-size spiral binder. Make sure you store it in a watertight container (a reclosable sandwich bag is perfect) and keep it on your boat, so you can make or check on entries any time you're aboard.

The following is a list of the basic data you should enter into your log. If you organize your log in chronological order, you will be able to quickly locate any event according to the time it occurred.

Record of Maintenance and Repairs

Being able to look at a single record and tell what has been maintained or repaired on your engine is a valuable asset. A proper record details the kind of work done, the date on which the work was done, the engine hour meter reading when the work was done, and the cost. This information also will help you perform maintenance when it should be done, instead of when you happen to think of it. A proper log also provides space for comments, both yours and a mechanic's, perhaps regarding the cause of a specific problem or the likelihood of future problems.

It's important to note that there is only one yardstick by which to measure everything that happens to your outboard and that's **engine hours**. There are some cases when a simple chronological interval (days or months) might dictate the need for work or maintenance, but it's far more likely that the determining factor will be the number of hours on the engine since the last service. If your boat is not equipped with an hour meter for each engine, either install one or have one installed immediately. The cost shouldn't exceed $50 per engine and the benefit is well worth the price.

Maintenance and Repair Log				
Date	**Work done**	**Engine hours**	**Cost**	**Remarks**
9/10/89	—	—	—	passage St. Lucie to Miami
9/12/89	spark plug change	4294	$62.30	Steve's Marine
9/21/92	removed fish line from lower unit	4330	—	self
9/30/92	new lower unit seal	4360	$111.40	Steve's Marine
10/20/92	Winter layup: fog cylinders, fuel stabilizers	4366	$94.60	didn't change lower unit
10/22/92	paint touch-up	4366	—	self; need recoat in spring
4/10/93	spring launch	4366	$88.40	propeller straightened

Figure 9-1 Sample logs *(continued on following pages)*.

Daily Engine Log			
Date	10/21/90		
Engine hours	412-440		
Fuel consumption	approx. 135 gal.		
Distance traveled	approx. 70 miles		
Gauges after warm-up			
IDLE RPM	**WATER PRESS.**	**ENG. TEMP.**	**VOLTS**
750	40 psi	175	14.5
Observations	hard starting		

Daily Engine Log			
Date	10/24/90		
Engine hours	440-443		
Fuel consumption	approx. 60 gal.		
Distance traveled	approx. 20 miles		
Gauges after warm-up			
IDLE RPM	**WATER PRESS.**	**ENG. TEMP.**	**VOLTS**
750	40 psi	175	14.5
Observations	none		

Daily Engine Log			
Date	10/29/90		
Engine hours	443-449		
Fuel consumption	approx. 35 gal.		
Distance traveled	approx. 20 miles		
Gauges after warm-up			
IDLE RPM	**WATER PRESS.**	**ENG. TEMP.**	**VOLTS**
750	40 psi	175	14.5
Observations	tune-up at 443 hours; starts fine		

Record of Fuel Consumption

Fuel consumption is another significant index of engine health. When fuel consumption increases, there's always a reason. It might be a heavier load, higher operating speeds, wear, or a faulty component. Unless you have a **fuel flow meter** on board, you'll need to calculate your fuel mileage by combining estimates of average speed, distance traveled, time underway, and fuel used inferred from how much it takes to top off your tank. Do all your estimates in your logbook so you'll have a record of this data. Admittedly this method produces a less than totally precise figure, but it gives one that is sufficiently accurate to be meaningful. If you're proficient at dead reckoning (getting a fix by estimating time, course, and speed), your estimation of total fuel consumption is likely to be surprisingly accurate.

Gauge Readings

You should make note of the readings of your most important gauges at start-up, again when the engine has reached operating temperature, and just before you shut it down. Among the parameters to note are idle speed, cooling-water pressure (water pressure gauges are becoming more prevalent in outboards), cooling-water temperature, and even battery voltage.

Obviously, you can carry this kind of thing so far that you'll never leave the dock, but even a complete inventory should take no more than a couple of minutes. To save time and space, use shorthand. For instance, if your engine produces 30 pounds of water pressure at idle and 40 pounds at wide-open throttle, you could write it: water pres 30 idle / 40 WOT.

The purpose of accumulating all this data is to establish an operating baseline, a list of criteria that constitute the normal operating characteristics of your engine. Such a list can be particularly valuable when you have to call a mechanic, but it also can be valuable by establishing an operational trend. For instance, if you look at your log over the last 100 hours and note that at the beginning your engine typically ran at 140°F and today it runs at 165°F, you'd have reason to be concerned. Such an increase wouldn't be sufficient alone to alarm most mechanics, nor would it trip an alarm system. Yet if engine load or operating speed hasn't changed drastically, you'd have to suspect the possibility of a cooling system problem.

Observations

As we'll see in subsequent chapters, you can tell a great deal about the state of your engine by observing certain physical signs, such as the color of its exhaust, the smoothness with which it idles and runs, how easy or difficult it is to start, the presence of oil on the engine or in the pan, and even the noises it makes.

After you've spent a few hours at the wheel you'll develop a feel for your engine, just as commercial boaters do, and you'll know when something "just doesn't seem right." Whatever observations you make about the way your propulsion system operates are important, if not at the moment, then as indicators of future trends. Write them down; some day they'll come in handy.

Ambient Temperature and Humidity

You can't properly interpret all the raw data noted above unless you know the **ambient** (outside your boat) **conditions**. Why? Because both temperature and humidity have a direct effect on how your engine operates. If you can't remember how cold it was when you noted that the engine was hard to start, the observation is far less meaningful. Likewise if you don't recall that when your engine was operating at 170°F you were in the Bahamas and the water temperature was 88°F, that observation has little meaning.

How do you get such information? The easiest way is simply to tune your VHF to a weather channel (which you should do anyway before you start any day aboard a boat) and listen to the NOAA reports, which periodically provide current air temperature and humidity, and usually also water temperature, which is important because it directly affects the operating temperature of an outboard.

All things being equal, the higher the ambient air temperature, the less horsepower your engine will produce. Since hot air is less dense, less oxygen reaches the combustion chamber per stroke.

Again you can record this information quickly in shorthand. If the air temperature is 90°F, the humidity is 80 percent, and the water temperature is 86°F, write AT90 / H80 / WT86. By the way, this information can be valuable when planning a cruise or fishing in familiar waters.

10

The Daily Checklist

Yes, it's a pain. You'd much rather just fire up that outboard and head off into the sunrise. You've dealt with enough hassles during the week; now's the time to relax. But don't. Just take a few minutes—that's all it takes—to make a few crucial checks. Those few minutes are essential to your preventative maintenance program and they will help ensure that your trip really will be hassle-free. Make yourself a short checklist, including the following items, and post it in a prominent place or in your log, so you don't forget.

Conduct a General Survey

Pull the engine cowling off and take a quick look around for signs of trouble, perhaps a pool of oil or water in the pan, encrustation of salt, missing paint, or something loose. Grab some of the wires, hoses, and external components and shake them to make sure they're secure. Make sure the V-belts (if so equipped) are tight. Look for signs of **weeping** around hoses and gaskets. Check for loose or worn wiring, especially spark plug wires. Squeeze hoses; if they feel mushy, they probably need replacement.

Check Your Battery's Electrolyte Level

If your batteries are difficult to reach this can be a real task. You may have to resort to a mirror and flashlight to get a good reading, but even if you must, don't skip this checkpoint. Make sure you know what the proper electrolyte level is; too much can be as bad as too little. A good rule of thumb is that the level should be about halfway between the top of the plates and the top of the battery. And while you're there, check that the battery is securely mounted, that there is no sign of fluid around it (an indication of a cracked battery case), and that the terminals are not corroded, loose, or dirty. Be careful; battery electrolyte is an acid that can harm you as well as your boat.

Log It

Write down the results of your checks in your log, even if everything is normal. Just knowing precisely when you last checked over your engine and precisely what you did can be a valuable advantage in the battle to keep your boat running smoothly.

The Daily Checklist: A Summary

❑	**Physical Exam**	Look for signs of loose or leaking components; check V-belts; look for loose parts in pan, frayed belts, soft hoses, or anything out of the ordinary.
❑	**Battery**	Check electrolyte level, mountings, and for signs of leaking.
❑	**Log**	Whatever action you take, note it in the log.

The Periodic Checklist

For day-to-day operation, the simple daily checklist detailed in the previous chapter is sufficient, but every 30 days or 20 hours of engine time, you should spend a little more time on your engine checking things with a closer eye. Even this more thorough perusal should take only a little of your time—maybe 20 minutes.

Before you start, you'll need a few simple tools. One of the most important is a **flashlight**, preferably one that throws a small, high-intensity beam. Also helpful are a **flat-blade screwdriver** and an **adjustable wrench**.

Periodic checks are best conducted when the engine has sat idle overnight and is cold. You'll be reaching around and touching many of the components, which will be hot if the engine's been running. Bring along a note pad, or better yet, your **logbook**, so you can record your observations.

Check Your Battery's State of Charge

You'll be checking the fluid level in your battery again, but this time you'll be more thorough. The syringe-like **hydrometer**, which will indicate the state of charge in each battery cell, is the tool of choice here. This is important because your battery may read 12 volts or higher on a voltmeter and yet one cell may be significantly weaker than the others, pointing toward trouble down the road. Even the best hydrometers (those that compensate for temperature) shouldn't cost more than $20 and are simple to use. Just follow the instructions that come with each one.

Check the Plumbing

At this point you'll begin a more thorough check of your engine and boat. The first things you should check are hoses and clamps. Squeeze the hoses. A good hose should be firm and resilient, but one that has broken down will feel mushy and collapse easily under pressure; it should be replaced. Use your flashlight to look for signs of peeling, cracking, or other external indications of breakdown.

Test clamps with your screwdriver to ensure they're tight. Tighten loose ones carefully because these clamps strip easily. Don't forget to check the fuel and oil (if so equipped) hoses that pass through the engine pan.

Check the Electrical System

Next check all electrical wiring, with special attention to **terminals** and **connections**. Check for looseness by pulling gently on the wire or plug—you'd rather have it come apart here than somewhere out in the water. Make temporary repairs with twist connectors and electrician's tape; permanent repairs require clamp-style electrical connectors or soldered junctions covered with heat-sensitive shrink wrap.

Selectively tighten terminals with your screwdriver. Look for dangling wires and support them at closely spaced intervals either with tape or with tie-wraps. Note signs of chafing where wiring passes through bulkheads or around metal components. Any loss of insulation, even if the wire isn't exposed, demands repair and preventative measures to avoid a repeat loss.

Check the high-tension spark plug wires, those leading from the coils to the spark plugs. *Do not pull them away from the spark plugs as this will weaken the terminals.* Instead, grasp each firmly and wiggle it, looking for signs of looseness or weakness. Also look for signs of frayed insulation, and make sure all wires are supported and clear of any hot engine parts.

Check Fuel Lines and Priming Bulb

Next turn your attention to the rubber fuel line. Trace it back from the engine as far as you can looking for abrasions, breaks, loose fittings, or leaks. (Remember that gasoline evaporates quickly so your only clue may be odor from the residue.) Check as far as you can visually using your flashlight, then rely on feel. Any rough spot on the line is suspect. Grope around in the boat carefully; loose strands of fiberglass and exposed screw heads can wreak havoc on your hands.

Take time to examine the priming bulb too. It should be free of cracks, firm, and resilient but not pliable or gooey. If it collapses easily under pressure, replace it.

Check Your Engine's Physical Condition

Last checks on your visual inventory are the engine mounts, located on the outboard bracket. Look for any signs of looseness, hardening, or cracking. Next check your engine's principal components to make sure they're all tight. This is also a good time to check **V-belts** for signs of **glazing**. Less frequently—about every 90 days—check each of your engine's zinc anodes. Remember, these are supposed to wear away, but if they get much below half gone you should replace them.

Clean Up

Leave your engine as clean and free of oil and grease as possible. A clean engine makes it easier to spot leaks and other trouble spots. Likewise touch up any chipped paint or bare metal with an approved paint designed to withstand high temperatures. Not only will it make your engine look nicer, it also will help resist corrosion and make real problems easier to spot.

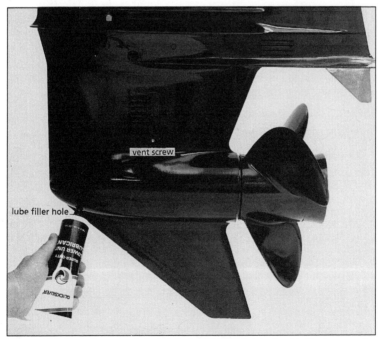

Figure 11-1 Part of your periodic check should include lube level in the lower unit. When the drive is vertical, oil should be at the level of the vent hole. (Courtesy Mercury Marine)

The Drive Unit

Now turn your attention to the drive unit itself. There are only four check points here, but they are important. First, check the level of the lower unit lube oil. In most drive units this means unscrewing a plug with a screwdriver and making sure some either dribbles out or you can at least feel it with your finger. Be careful! There are usually two plugs. The lower is for draining only; you want the upper one.

At the same time note the color of the lube oil. If it's cloudy, you've got a leak, probably around the propeller seal. Have it fixed immediately or you'll soon have serious drive unit problems. Finally, screw the plug back in and make sure it's tight.

Second, check the condition of the zincs you can't see, usually the one up inside the lower unit, in front of the propeller. You also may have a large zinc "brick" up under the transom bracket. As long as each is intact you're OK. Look for trends. If one of your zincs has worn away a lot since your last check, it's a sure sign you've got a corrosion problem and should investigate.

Third, look for nicks and scrapes on the drive unit. Touch up any with approved touch-up paint to prevent them from turning into corrosion problems.

Fourth, make a general inspection, looking for leakage around the trim cylinders, loose parts or wires, or any obvious damage.

Finally, make sure to note any observations of things you found, whether you repaired them or not, in your log.

The Periodic Checklist: A Summary

❏	**Battery**	Check electrolyte level, mountings, leakage, and state of charge in each cell with a hydrometer.
❏	**Hoses**	Look for leaks or deterioration (hoses should be firm, not mushy); check for loose or corroded clamps.
❏	**Electrical**	Test for loose terminals, check for sealed connections; look for frayed wiring and worn insulation.
❏	**Fuel Lines**	Check hard lines; look for abrasion on soft lines; look for weeping at connections. Check all clamped lines for tightness and integrity.
❏	**Priming Bulb**	Look for cracks. Test for firmness and resiliency. If easily collapsed under pressure, replace.
❏	**Engine Mounts**	Look for signs of looseness, cracks, and other wear.

❏	**Miscellaneous**	Check tightness of all components.
❏	**V-Belts**	Look for fraying or glazing; check for proper tightness (½ inch of play).
❏	**Zincs**	Replace any that are more than half gone.
❏	**Leaks**	Check pan, hoses and lines, gaskets, all mating surfaces.
❏	**Drive unit**	Check lube oil level and color. Check and touch up nicks. Check condition of zincs. Conduct overall examination.
❏	**Log**	Note anything out of the ordinary in your log.

From Start-Up to Shutdown

The few minutes immediately after you start an outboard and just before you shut it down are among the crucial times in its life. How you treat it during that time will determine how long your outboard lasts.

Start-Up

After you've completed your preliminary checks, you're ready to start your engine. You'll notice that many captains pump the throttle a few times to "prime" the engine before turning the key. Although it may look authoritative, it is a waste of time and actually may make the engine harder to start by overfueling it. In most cases, moving the throttle lever all the way forward and back to neutral once is all that's needed. This movement also closes the choke plate if it's open.

Under normal circumstances, when you push the throttle lever forward it automatically shifts the outboard into forward. You'll want to open the throttle slightly while keeping the outboard in neutral. (Thanks to a safety mechanism, if you try to start your engine while it's in gear it will not crank.)

How you do this depends upon the make of control you use. If you have a Mercury/Quicksilver, you'll probably find a black button to push in the middle of the lever axis. On many other controls you first pull the base of the lever out, then push the lever forward. If you're not sure how to advance the throttle in neutral, check your owner's manual.

Opening the throttle will give the engine a little more fuel and usually will make starting easier. Don't pump the throttle and don't open the throttle too far. About one-third of the way is usually sufficient.

Any farther and you'll either flood the engine or the engine will roar to life, which causes undue wear and tear.

With the throttle open and your hand on it, turn the key and crank the engine over. Keep your hand on the throttle so that when the engine starts you can throttle it back if it roars to life. Your goal should be a fast-idle (which your car does automatically) of about 1500 r.p.m.

Once the engine is running, leave it alone. Now is a good time to untie lines, pull in fenders, and do all the last-minute things you must do before shoving off. If you have small children around (or irresponsible adults) it's a good idea to have someone tend the throttle while you're busy so no accidents happen. After about two minutes, pull the throttle back into neutral. The engine should drop back to idle speed, between 700 and 900 r.p.m. You're now ready to get under way.

If you wait until your engine idles down before you place your outboard into gear you'll save a lot of wear and tear. Likewise, if you idle away from the dock for a minute or so you'll allow all the gears to become fully lubricated and you'll reduce wear. Above all, remember that the highest wear rates in outboards and drives occur when they are cold and the lubrication system is not yet working at maximum efficiency. Take it easy and you'll extend the life of your outboard.

Trimming your drive all the way down or "in" will help the boat plane more quickly and reduce engine load. Depress the trim button until you hear the hydraulic pump strain (it's OK; it's designed to do that), make sure the wheel is straight, then apply power smoothly and steadily until your boat is on plane. Once there, throttle back or up to your desired cruising speed.

Don't drive your boat at speeds between hull speed and planing if you can avoid it. If your boat is running in an exaggerated nose-high attitude in spite of having the drive trimmed all the way in, either put it up on plane or throttle it back to a speed where you're running more level. Running just off plane places undue strain on your engine and drive. It also creates an unnecessarily large wake that can damage other boats and

Figure 12-1 Many engine controls, such as this one for two engines, have integral switches for trimming or tilting the engine. To advance the dual throttles while keeping the engines in neutral you must pull on each base.

make other boaters uncomfortable. Your rule of thumb, regardless of where you run, always should be to minimize wake, even if there doesn't seem to be anyone around. Wakes can travel many miles and still cause damage, and a large wake is a sign of a boat that is running inefficiently and out of trim. For your sake and others', *always* minimize your wake.

Choosing a Cruising Speed

The next question is at what speed you should cruise. It is widely accepted that the faster you run an engine, the faster it wears. Fuel efficiency—and therefore range—is the product of many factors, including hull form, but as a general rule an outboard will run most efficiently between 4000 and 4200 r.p.m., mainly because this is where its induction system is most efficient. Another guideline is that the greater the disparity between speed and mileage, the greater the engine load. The greater the engine load, the higher the wear rate.

In selecting the best cruise speed, you need to use optimum trim. This is generally a matter of trial and error, since optimum trim is dependent upon variables such as weight, weight distribution, and water conditions. Once on plane, the best way to trim is to push the trim button to the "UP" position until you hear the engine speed up (assuming you're not moving the throttle), then trim it down just a tad until the engine speed drops back. The increase in speed you hear is the propeller loosing bite in the water, and what you're aiming for is maximum bite with the bow as high as you can get it without losing control or visibility. When the bow is high, the water drag on the hull is minimized and your boat will run faster and more efficiently. You should notice significantly less steering torque when the drive is properly trimmed.

Shutting Down

The rule here is simple, but often ignored: Give the engine just a little time to cool down before shutting it off. The most prudent course is to reverse the start-up procedure: Pull into the dock or mooring, throttle the engine back to idle, and go about your anchoring/mooring chores for a minute while your engine cools down. Then you can safely shut it off.

Many boaters can't resist that last punch of the throttle to speed up the engine before switching off the key. When they do, all they're doing is wearing away a little more engine and shooting a little more raw fuel into the cylinders that won't burn completely. Eventually the unburned fuel will leave deposits in the cylinder.

PART THREE

How to Care for Your Outboard

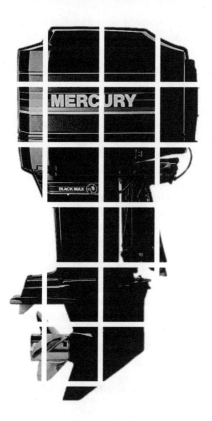

Selecting and Changing Oil

Note: This chapter is not meant to contradict in any way the maintenance schedule and manufacturer's recommendations included in your owner's manual. On the contrary, it is complementary, and is intended to help you better fulfill those guidelines.

Outboard Oil

Like the oil used in four-cycle engines, that used in your outboard is designed primarily as a lubricant, maintaining a film between critical mechanical parts. But unlike four-cycle oil, two-cycle oil is burned in the combustion chamber, so it must be specifically designed to burn as cleanly and completely as possible. Otherwise it will leave harmful deposits that will accelerate wear.

Choosing the right kind of outboard oil is simple, much simpler than choosing oil for your car. The only thing you need to look for is an approved rating. Two are acceptable: TC-W or TC-WII, which is a slightly more advanced version. (The TC stands for two-cycle and the W stands for water-cooled.) As long as the oil you select bears one of these ratings on its label you can be assured of getting proper engine protection.

If you manually mix oil and gasoline, you'll find the best way to get maximum mixing is to pour the oil in first, then add the gasoline. If you do it in reverse, you may find some of the oil lingers near the surface. Remember to check for your engine's recommended ratio. Fifty to one is most common, but some newer engines can run on 100:1. Always err on the side of too much oil and, unless you make a gross error, there won't be any adverse effect. Too little oil, however, could spell disaster.

Whether you mix oil manually or pour it into a separate tank to be mixed by a pump, remember that oil does eventually degrade if left untouched. Oxygen, moisture, and other contaminants can cause it to oxidize, loosing some of its lubricative qualities. Consequently, try not to leave oil stored in an open or vented container for longer than eight weeks. If it will be left untouched for longer than that—say for winter lay-up—it's better to empty the old oil and refill come spring or whenever you're ready to use the engine again.

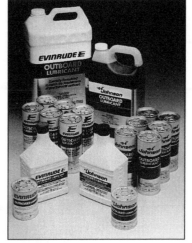

Figure 13-1 Outboard engine oil is available in many sizes. Whichever brand you choose, make sure the oil is rated TC-W or TC-WII. (Courtesy OMC)

Drive Unit Oil

Like your stern drive engine, your drive unit also needs a supply of oil to keep its moving parts (mainly gears) from wearing out. This oil, however, is totally different in weight and constitution from engine oil. This is gear oil, a heavy-weight lube specifically designed to coat and protect gears.

Check your owner's manual for drive oil recommendations. Chances are your unit will require "hypoid" oil. If you want to play it safe you can simply purchase the oil sold under the name of your drive's builder. There are also many fine after-market oils that are equally effective. Just check the manufacturer's specification to make sure you pick the oil your drive unit needs.

Under most operating conditions, drive oil need only be changed once each season. However, as noted previously, you should periodically check the oil level in your drive and its clarity, which will tell you if it has become contaminated with water. These checks are important because if there's a problem with leakage between oil and water you'll likely never know unless you see it manifested in a lower oil level or cloudy oil. Left alone, either low oil or water-contaminated oil will ruin your drive unit.

Caring for Fuel

Gasoline is a complex substance with a number of important properties, but only a few concern us. One is octane, a measure of the fuel's ability to resist ignition before the spark plug fires. Generally, the higher the compression ratio, the higher the octane required to prevent pre-ignition. Fortunately, today most engines run just fine on regular-octane fuel.

If you have an older, high-compression or special high-performance engine, you may need to purchase higher octane fuel. One sign that your engine needs higher octane fuel can be **spark knock** or **pinging** when it's under load. Some knock is acceptable, but severe, loud, continuous knock is cause for concern. Knock also can indicate that the ignition timing is out of adjustment. If your engine constantly knocks and higher octane fuel doesn't seem to help, better check its timing and **dwell**, the distance between the breaker points.

Another property of gasoline that's important to boaters is the presence of alcohol. Alcohol can come from a variety of sources, such as grains and wood, and refiners usually add it to extend gasoline and reduce costs. Alcohol has two properties that concern boaters: (1) It can attract and combine with water in a damp environment, meaning less power and more fuel system corrosion, and (2) it can also attack certain kinds of synthetic rubber fuel lines, usually those in older fuel systems.

If you have an older boat you should be especially attentive during your regular check of fuel-line components. Look for sticky or soft lines, or lines that remain depressed when you squeeze them. Replace them with new fuel lines, nearly all of which are now rated for use with alcohol fuels.

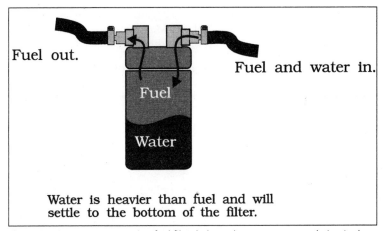

Fuel out.

Fuel and water in.

Fuel

Water

Water is heavier than fuel and will settle to the bottom of the filter.

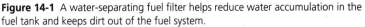

Figure 14-1 A water-separating fuel filter helps reduce water accumulation in the fuel tank and keeps dirt out of the fuel system.

The best defense against moisture is to keep your fuel tank full when you're not using your boat. This reduces condensation and water accumulation in the fuel tank. You can add an **auxiliary water-separating fuel filter**, available from most engine and boat dealers, and after-market suppliers. Such a filter also keeps dirt out of your fuel system.

That brings us to gasoline's final important property: cleanliness. The carburetor contains a number of small passages that easily clog with even the tiniest particulate matter. Abrasive material, such as sand and grit, that makes its way into the combustion chamber may not be destroyed during combustion and could end up grinding away rings and cylinder walls.

Many newer outboards have a small cleanable filter under the engine cover just after the fuel line passes through the lower engine pan. Its capacity is small and it's really designed as a filter of last resort. For that reason, you should have a large canister-type filter somewhere between the engine and the fuel tank to offer real protection. Better yet, make it a water-separating fuel filter like that described above. Most filter elements are good for one boating season, and replacement cost is typically less than $10. Once again, cheap insurance.

If your fuel filter does become clogged, your engine will either begin to miss as it starves for fuel or, more likely, just quit. The only solution is to replace the contaminated fuel filter, which is a good reason to always carry a spare. In most installations, you will have to fill the fuel filter cartridge with fuel before attaching it to prevent the engine from sucking air.

If your filters are constantly clogging, your problem may not be at the pump; it may be in your fuel tank. Most tanks are designed with the **fuel pick-up** a few inches off the bottom of the tank. This leaves a dead area in which dirt and heavy contaminants can accumulate without being drawn into the fuel line. If you have an older boat or one with a lot of hours on it, your fuel tank may have a layer of contaminant on its bottom that has built up sufficiently to reach the fuel pick-up. The only solution is to have the tank either replaced or cleaned. That's a job for a professional.

Additives

There are dozens of salesmen out there with "miracle" fuel additives that supposedly will double your mileage. Approach these with a healthy dose of skepticism. In the most operating environments no fuel additive is necessary, and in some cases one actually may be harmful. There is, however, one notable exception.

Gasoline is fine as long as it's being used, or at least being moved around. When it's left idle for some time, bad things can happen. Moisture and air can combine with it to create oxidation, gum, and varnish that can clog your fuel system.

The solution is to add a **fuel stabilizer** whenever you believe your boat will sit undisturbed for longer than a month. Fuel stabilizers are formulated to preserve the fuel and prevent oxidation. They come in various types and formulations, not all of which are necessarily good for your engine. The best place to turn for advice concerning a fuel stabilizer for your outboard is the engine manufacturer or distributor. Outboard Marine Corporation, Mercury Marine, and MDR all have reputable fuel stabilizers. Do not rely solely upon advertising claims or buy simply what is being sold at the boatyard; there's a lot of snake oil on the market today, some of which can end up taking a big bite out of your wallet while failing to live up to its promises.

Caring for the
Ignition System

I've said it before in this book and I'll say it again: The weakest link in your outboard is its ignition system. That's why you must service and maintain it with diligence. If you don't, you can almost count on problems. Ignition system maintenance comes in two parts: low voltage and high voltage.

Low-Voltage Maintenance

Low-voltage maintenance starts at the battery and ends at the coils. Every connection must be clean, tight, and dry or you'll have a current leak. *Clean* means each pole and connector must be bright—otherwise you do not have optimum connection. You can brighten poles and connectors with a little fine sandpaper. *Tight* is self-explanatory. A loose connection means a weak connection, and weak connections mean trouble.

Dry means, simply, no moisture. That means you must exclude moisture (and therefore air) by covering each connection (including splices) with an impermeable coating. This could be a special ignition spray or heat-sensitive shrink wrap. It does not mean merely using slide-in, crimp, or twist connectors, nor does it mean the application (in any amount) of just tape or silicone sealant. Every connection must be air- and moisture-tight or you are sure to have problems.

High-Voltage Maintenance

High-voltage maintenance starts at the coil and ends at the spark plugs. Remember, you're dealing with as much as 40,000 volts—and current that's ever ready to take the shortest way home. If there is any

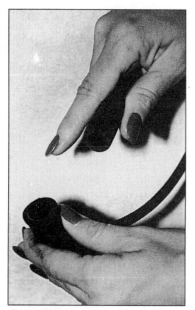

Figure 15-1 The spark plug wires are the critical links in the ignition system. Check wire insulation for erosion and make sure all connectors are tight at each end.

gap or opening to the air, high-voltage current will jump it and go to ground, and the spark plug won't fire.

The most critical links in the system are the spark plug wires, including their connectors at each end. There can be no exposed or eroded insulation, and all connectors must be tight. The boots that fit over the terminals at the coil, distributor, and spark plugs must be supple and clean. If they're hard they'll crack and let in air. Air means moisture and moisture means a short circuit. If the boots are dirty, the dirt will conduct the high-voltage current to ground and the spark plugs won't fire.

If you have any doubt about the condition of your spark plug wires, replace them. If one is bad, the rest are probably soon to go. Opinions vary, but most mechanics like to replace a spark plug wire set every other boating season. The cost shouldn't be more than $50, and you can easily install them yourself.

Plugs, Points, and Condenser

Finally we come to the parts everyone knows about: those that comprise the famous tune-up. Of course we're speaking of the plugs, points, and condenser. (If you've got an outboard with electronic or capacitor discharge ignition, you're off the hook for the points and condenser.) As for points, know that the gap between them must be very accurate. An error of just a few thousandths of an inch will mean arcing, pitting, additional wear, and eventual misfiring. If you can't set the points accurately (and many of us cannot), let a mechanic do it. This is one of the most critical adjustments in the ignition system. It's got to be right.

If you do install and adjust your own points, consider buying an electronic dwell meter, which is used to measure the distance between breaker points. It can tell you far more accurately than mechanical feeler gauges whether your points are set right. A dwell meter is easy to use; just follow the manufacturer's directions that come with it. And by all means, remember to tighten the screws that hold the points securely. One of the most common ignition-related problems—believe it or not—is points that vibrate loose and stop the engine.

You might be tempted to save money by purchasing a small file and filing the ridges and peaks on the points, then resetting them; *don't!* Points are cheap. Install a new pair at the beginning of every boating season. Period! Always install a new condenser with the new points.

The story on spark plugs is not as straightforward as the story on points and the condenser. With unleaded fuel, spark plugs can easily last three or four boating seasons. If, however, you decide to stretch out their life, you must pull them once a year and re-set the gap between the electrodes. (Check your owner's manual for recommended clearance.) While you're at it, clean off the plug tips with a bronze or relatively soft wire brush, and clean the white insulator and nut head with a dry, clean cloth. (Don't use solvent as it will leave a film and attract more grease and dirt.)

Of course, you could be on the safe side and simply replace your spark plugs at the end of every season. That, in my opinion, is the best approach.

Whichever option you choose, make sure you remove and install the spark plug wire carefully or you'll have a bad connection and all your work will be for naught. Once the connector and boot are on the plug, wiggle them to make sure they're snug.

Doing It Yourself

For a variety of reasons, including saving money and the simple joy of doing it yourself, a lot of boaters would prefer to do the chores on their outboards. Unfortunately, many shy away from the task, not because of laziness but because of concern that the job may be too difficult. In truth, the procedures involved in maintaining an outboard are simple—even simpler than those used in maintaining your automobile.

We've already discussed how to choose the right oil; buying the proper two-cycle oil is crucial to the life of your engine. Since your outboard burns oil in its cylinders, you don't have to worry about periodic oil and filter changes—like you do in your car—but that doesn't mean you have no oil-related maintenance.

Of course, I'm referring to the oil (or more properly, lube) in your outboard's lower unit. Regular maintenance on this unit is crucial but thankfully simple. You should change the lower unit drive oil at least once a year; more often if you put more than 200 hours on your engine. The procedure is simple: Make sure the drive is warm so the oil will flow, trim it until it's roughly vertical, place a pan beneath it to catch the oil, remove the top plug (the one by which you checked the oil level) to provide a place for air to enter the oil chamber, then remove the bottom plug. Give the lube plenty of time to drain, then replace the lower screw.

Examine the oil carefully for signs of contamination, such as discoloration, iridescence, or cloudiness. Then replace the lower plug and prepare to refill the unit.

Most drive lube comes in a tube, the nozzle of which fits into the fill hole. Cut off the end of this nozzle, insert it into the fill hole, and squeeze until you see oil begin to drip back out, indicating the drive is full. Insert and tighten the plug, wipe off the drive, and properly dispose of the old lube.

Other drive service involves touching up paint and replacing zincs that are more than half gone. Also note that if your outboard operates in salt water and its zincs show virtually no wear, it may be a sign they aren't doing their job. Look for corrosion in any component that does not have a good connection to the rest of the drive. Make sure you look carefully for subsurface paint bubbling, a sign that corrosion has entered one place and is traveling between alloy and paint. These areas should be scraped clean, primed, and painted. Never paint or wax zincs.

If your outboard will be out of the water for a day or longer, now is a good time to scrub the exterior with soap and water to remove salt and contaminants. (You should try to hose off the outboard after each use, particularly if you run in salt water.) You may want to apply a coat of protective wax to protect the drive even further.

If you're running in polluted or salt water, this is also a good time to flush the interior cooling passages with fresh water using a special adapter that clamps around the raw-water intakes, which are just forward of and above the propeller on either side.

At this time you may also want to remove the propeller and shine a light inside to check on the condition of the internal zinc in the lower unit. Make sure to reinstall the propeller with a new lock washer or cotter key and grease the propeller shaft so that it will be easy to remove the prop next time. Also check the condition of the propeller. Repair any nicks, dents, or other imperfections. A damaged propeller may be out of balance, which can cause vibration and eventually ruin your propeller seals.

Make sure the bright steel hydraulic rams on the trim cylinders have a coat of oil. They depend on frequent use to maintain the oily coating. If the coating degrades the rams will rust, damaging the seals inside and allowing the hydraulic fluid to leak out.

Now pull the engine cowling, then hose off the engine with a light spray to remove salt, dirt, and grease. After it dries, spray all metal components with a light coat of lightweight oil such as WD-40. You don't need much. Also wipe down the spark plug wires with a protective spray, and check for loose connections, particularly at the spark plug boots. Look for any signs that water is accumulating in the engine pan; that could mean a deteriorated engine cowling gasket.

Fuel Filters

As we noted before, many new outboards have a small fuel filter with a cleanable element under the engine cover. In most cases it will have a translucent body, so you can check for contamination without opening it. If you have any doubt, open the unit, pull out the filter screen, and examine it for debris.

Separate exterior fuel filters usually require changing once a year. There are a number of types—spin-on, cartridge, and in-line—and all are easy to remove and install. However, when you install a new fuel filter you should, if possible, fill it with clean fuel to prevent the carburetor from sucking air at start-up.

Be obsessively careful about fuel leaks. Gasoline is extremely dangerous. Always make a thorough check for fuel leaks after installing a new fuel filter. At the same time, check all connections, fuel and oil (if equipped with oil injection) lines, and squeeze bulb for leaks and deterioration. If they're soft, gooey, or stay depressed when you pinch them, they're probably degraded from alcohol in the fuel and must be replaced.

Ignition System

Anyone with a modicum of mechanical ability should be able to remove, clean, gap, and reinstall a set of spark plugs, or gap and install a new set. Just remember to gap them carefully according to the engine manufacturer's recommendations, and don't over-tighten them.

Once a year, as part of your ignition service, you also should check the engine's ignition timing. This can be a difficult job for a novice, as it requires accurate use of a timing light. If you've never used a timing light, have someone show you how to connect one and use it, preferably on your engine. You can get general guidance from a number of automotive books.

Other Service

Some older outboards may have grease fittings or other lubrication points, such as at the throttle linkage and bracket pivot points. Check your owner's manual for specifications. As a basic guideline, keep all movable links and cables well-lubricated so they move easily.

If you live where temperatures fall below freezing you may have to prepare your outboard for winter lay-up. This is another procedure you either can do yourself or leave to a mechanic. Basically, winterization involves removing any water from the engine cooling system, shutting off the fuel supply and running the engine until it quits to get all the fuel out of the fuel system, topping off the fuel tanks to prevent condensation, and adding a fuel stabilizer. You also should pull each spark plug and spray the plug hole with a rust preventative or special protective fog, which you can buy from your local dealer or marine supply store. Outboard Marine Corporation, Mercury Marine and MDR all market spray protectives. For more specific recommendations, check your engine owner's manual.

How to Choose and Deal with a Mechanic

Selecting a mechanic is like selecting a physician: You don't really want one but you know you need one, and you're unsure about how to choose one because you don't know much about the discipline. This is why doctors—and mechanics—named Adams fare better than those named Zimmerman: The natural tendency is to rely on alphabetical order when all else fails.

There are ways to tell good mechanics from bad, but shopping for the best deal is not one of them. There are plenty of good mechanics who charge a low hourly rate and just as many bad ones who charge a high hourly rate. If you find a mechanic that works cheap, he may be so incompetent that it takes him twice as long to do the job. We'll deal more with the financial aspects of mechanics in a moment. Right now, lets talk about choosing a good one.

The first rule of dealing with a mechanic is "Don't be intimidated." It's true, you probably know a lot less about engines and drives than he, but never forget that you're the one paying the bills—you should be in the driver's seat. Never be afraid to ask a mechanic anything or to challenge him when you're dissatisfied with his answer. If you learn just this one thing—deal with a mechanic from a position of strength and authority—you will have gone a long way toward getting your money's worth.

Once you start looking for a mechanic, your first source should be word of mouth. If you have a friend with an outboard-powered boat, ask if your friend is happy with his or her mechanic. If your friend's outboard is the same make as yours, so much the better. Also ask the yard foreman, the person who sold you the boat, and those whose boats are moored around you. If you get a rousing recommendation from any of them, check the guy out. If you get two or three opinions that agree, you're in real luck.

The next step should be to meet with the mechanic before you actually call him for work. Ideally, the meeting will take place at his shop so you can have a look around. Being a mechanic is a dirty job, but that doesn't preclude neatness. If he's a slob and his toolbox looks like a kid's toy chest, he's disorganized at best and a poor mechanic at worst. And if he doesn't have time to talk to you, forget him.

When you speak to a mechanic, ask him about his training and experience. Any factory training and certification is a big plus, although no guarantee of success. Recurrent training in specialized areas is a sign that he takes his profession seriously and wants to stay abreast of new developments.

Discuss your specific engine and boat with him, and note how he listens. A lot of mechanics have little or no respect for an owner, and you can tell that in the way they listen. Stay away from these people, no matter how expert they may seem, or they'll end up directing your life. If the mechanic expresses some familiarity with your engine or boat, that's a good sign. More important, however, is his overall attitude. Does he seem reasonable, interested, and fair-minded, as well as being competent?

In the end, you really need to know more about human nature than engines and drives to choose a mechanic. Don't be afraid to rely on your impressions and instincts. The truth is a good mechanic is hard to find, and finding one often is as much a matter of serendipity as forethought.

What's a Fair Fee?

Mechanics generally compute their charges one of two ways: One is the standard-rate method where, by referring to a book, a mechanic can tell how much time it should take (at least theoretically) to perform a certain job. He simply multiplies that time by his hourly rate and gets the estimated charges. If he gets the job done faster you still pay the estimated rate; if it takes longer he'll charge you more. The standard-rate method is most common in large shops.

The other method is simply to multiply how long it takes to actually complete the job by the hourly rate. This sounds simple, but there are variations on the theme. For instance, some mechanics show up at a job cold, with no parts and perhaps not even the correct tools. They then proceed to charge you for the time it takes them to travel to and from the shop or parts house and, if that weren't enough, they may even plug in a markup on the parts. Naturally, a mechanic legitimately could find he needs an unanticipated part or tool after getting into a job, but generally this bare-bones approach is a rip-off.

Evaluating Estimates and Invoices

You should be able to get firm estimates for most scheduled maintenance and for most common types of repairs. But understand that a
boat is not like a car: Every installation varies slightly. If it takes a mechanic longer to remove the powerhead from your outboard because
the boat's design doesn't allow full tilt range, you'll have to pay for it.
If, however, a mechanic refuses to give you any firm estimates for
scheduled maintenance, you probably should look for another mechanic.

Although it's probably too late to save you at this point, a look at a
mechanic's invoice can tell you a lot about the quality of his work.
Check the number of hours posted. It's normal to round off time, but if
he's rounding off 2½ hours to 3 hours, you're getting ripped off.

Note the prices for parts. This is where many mechanics really pad
their bills. If a price seems too high, don't hesitate to ask about it. If the
explanation seems inadequate, call a local parts house and verify the
cost. You have to expect some markup, but anything over 25 percent is
cause for questioning.

Another potential trouble spot is in the miscellaneous category,
sometimes referred to as "shop materials." Originally this was intended to cover incidentals, such as shop towels, grease, and miscellaneous chemicals, but often it develops into just another way to jack up
the bill. You shouldn't hesitate to ask about this charge either, particularly if it exceeds $25.

Don't be reticent about asking to see any old parts that were replaced. This is not being rude, it's just being a smart customer. If a raw-
water impeller looks perfectly fine to you, ask the mechanic to explain
why he replaced it. If his explanation seems implausible, don't pay for
it.

And finally, don't pay for any unauthorized work. It isn't unusual
for a mechanic to say, "I know we didn't talk about it but once I got
inside I thought this should be replaced." Tell him ahead of time to
speak to you before he does any work you haven't already specified.
Just making that statement will make him think twice about padding
the work.

Most mechanics are honest, hardworking individuals, but as in every other profession there are exceptions. Armed with a working
knowledge of your engine and drive, and a healthy dose of cynicism,
chances are you'll never have to worry about being someone's patsy.

Basic Tools and Spare Parts

This book is specifically designed for the layman, the boat owner who prefers to leave major engine work to an expert. But even the most uninvolved owner will need to carry a few well-chosen parts and tools on board, if only to get out of a jam. The tools should fit easily into a small toolbox and the parts should take up no more than a couple of square feet.

Tools

There are two ways to proceed in setting up a tool kit. You can simply go to one of the tool outlets like Sears, get one of the 100-piece mechanic's tool kits, and keep it aboard. That will certainly cover most of your needs, not to mention take up a lot of space. Or, you can pick only those tools you think you are most likely to need. In either case, purchase high-quality tools, not the kind you pull out of a bargain bin for 99 cents each. (Note that the recommendations that follow apply to your outboard; other tools may be necessary for the rest of your boat.)

A basic tool kit should begin with a socket wrench set, from ¼ to ¾ inch, along with a ratchet, a couple of drive extensions, and a universal joint. You'll note that socket sets come in a variety of drive sizes and in either deep or standard socket design. You'll probably get the most use from standard-depth sockets, and find the ½-inch drive is easiest to work with and store.

In addition to socket wrenches, bring along an 8-inch adjustable wrench. Many mechanics sneer at these but they've gotten a lot of boatmen out of many a jam. There's nothing wrong with an adjustable wrench as long as you buy a top-quality one. For smaller work, you

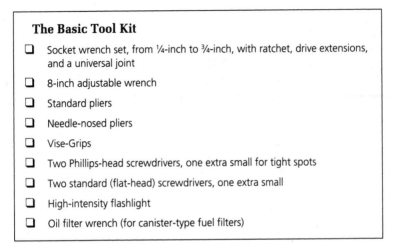

might consider a nut driver, a sort of screwdriver/mini-socket wrench combo, with sockets down to at least ¼ inch.

Three pairs of pliers are a good idea: a standard pair, a pair of needle-nosed pliers, and—perhaps the most versatile tool in your kit— a pair of Vise-Grips. A pair of offset long-handle pliers (sometimes called water-pump pliers) is optional.

Pack a set of standard and Phillips-head screwdrivers, including an extra-small version of each, and a high-intensity flashlight designated for work only. An oil-filter wrench is a good idea if you have a canister-type fuel filter.

This constitutes a basic tool kit, the kind needed to perform most of the basic maintenance procedures or emergency repairs. If you're planning on more extensive work, or if you just want to be prepared for any eventuality, you may also want to include a set of combination wrenches (box- and open-end), one or two cold chisels, a prick punch, a hydrometer, and a set of feeler gauges or a dwell meter. A quick check with your local engine distributor will also get you a list of specialized tools (and a shop manual) for your type and make of engine.

If you do your boating in salt water, take steps to ensure your tools won't corrode from the salt air. Look for a toolbox with a tight-fitting lid, or better, a gasketed cover. Wipe all tools down occasionally with an oil-soaked rag to help repel moisture.

In addition to tools, you'll want a few other items in your tool kit. Most important are a can of lightweight, all-purpose oil, such as WD-40, and rolls of both electrical and duct tape. A small piece of fine-grit sandpaper is handy for cleaning up metal surfaces and electrical contacts. Also include a small tube of silicone sealant. Effective in

Figure 18-1 If you do your boating in salt water, keep your tools in a box with a tight-fitting, gasket lid and wipe down tools with an oil-soaked rag to repel moisture and prevent corrosion.

stopping leakage, it also functions well as an all-purpose adhesive. Best of all, it's easily removable.

Other items worth bringing along are an assortment of hose clamps (stainless steel only, including the bolt), and an assortment of bolts, nuts, washers, and self-tapping screws. An inexpensive circuit tester can be a big help in tracking down electrical maladies. And don't forget that shop manual; even if you never intend to sit down and read it, you may find that some day you'll need it.

Parts

You have to make a basic philosophical decision up front regarding spare parts: Do you want to carry every conceivable part that could break during the course of a trip? Or can you be content to bring along only the essentials? If you're not likely to be more than a half-day's run from port (and parts), I suggest you conserve space and carry just the basics. These include at least one fuel filter, at least two quarts of two-cycle oil, and a tube of gear oil. Also important are at least one raw-water pump impeller (including gaskets) and an assortment of zincs.

Many boaters also bring along a set of spark plugs. If you do your

---

The Basic Parts Kit

❑   1 fuel filter

❑   2 quarts two-cycle oil

❑   1 tube of gear lube

❑   1 raw-water pump impeller with gaskets

❑   An assortment of zincs

❑   1 set of spark plugs

maintenance regularly, these shouldn't be necessary. Of course, they couldn't hurt. Plugs don't suddenly wear out, but their insulators could break and they could become fouled if the engine fails to start. If you bring them along consider pre-gapping them so you can install them quickly.

Whatever parts you bring should be rotated into use to prevent them from degrading in storage. For instance, if you keep a fuel filter on board, the next time you perform your scheduled maintenance use it and replace it with a new one. Likewise the spark plugs. That way all of your parts will be fresh and ready for use every time you need them. Keep all your parts in waterproof containers to prevent corrosion and mildew.

Basic Engine Troubleshooting

I can't possibly give you specific instructions on how to fix your outboard. Any attempt at that would be futile if for no other reason than even within the same brand, each model is slightly different from the other. Comprehensive troubleshooting instructions would be either prohibitively long or so vague as to be useless.

Instead, I'll concentrate on a brief philosophical discussion about the art of troubleshooting, and I'll give you a few basic questions to ask yourself before you call a mechanic. If you're looking for something more specific, purchase the shop manual for your particular outboard. Most include a comprehensive troubleshooting chart that can walk you through virtually any problem.

Despite the vast array of sophisticated testing equipment available, your senses remain your most valuable diagnostic tools; odd sounds or odors, hot surfaces, or the color of the engine's exhaust can announce problems long before they appear on gauges.

Get to know the sound of your engine. When you hear something out of the ordinary, pay attention. A loud knocking, for instance, could signal a bad connecting rod—or just an engine cover left ajar. A strong odor could indicate a fuel leak, an overheating engine, or an electrical problem. You often can locate the source of an overheating problem by feeling—with extreme caution—for hot and cold spots.

Your eyes can be helpful as well. One of the best ways to tell how an engine is running is by the color of its exhaust, an accurate diagnostic technique when used with certain limitations in mind. Remember that because a marine engine mixes water with its exhaust, the exhaust is more difficult to read than an automotive engine's.

Two exhaust colors indicate problems: black and blue. Black exhaust indicates either too much fuel or not enough air. Two possible explanations for black exhaust could be either a clogged air intake or an improperly adjusted fuel system. Blue smoke indicates that oil is burning in the combustion chamber, which is normal in a two-cycle engine. However, excessive smoke may mean you incorrectly measured oil or that your automatic oiling system isn't working. If left alone, excessive oil eventually will foul spark plugs and bring the engine to a halt.

The Troubleshooting Process

Troubleshooting is really nothing more than a logical process of elimination, but to do it well you must have at least a basic knowledge of how an engine works. If you've read this book you know enough about an outboard to troubleshoot it. Here are three simple questions to ask that probably will unearth almost any problem:

1. Have I Done All the Simple Things? If you remember only one lesson from this chapter, this is the one to remember: Your engine is basically reliable and durable, and it's unlikely that it will ever actually break. More often, the problem will be that you have overlooked some minor detail that has caused the engine to malfunction. There is an unalterable human desire to find a macro reason for a problem, when more often it's just a simple glitch that's put you out of service. Think small.

For instance, suppose your engine simply stops running. Before you suspect that the crankshaft has broken in two, walk yourself back through the most basic steps in starting. Is the key on? (Yes, you turned it on, but has it been turned off inadvertently?) Is the safety lanyard in place? Is there fuel in the tank? (The gauge says there is, but are you sure the fuel gauge is accurate or even working?) Is the fuel getting from the tank to the engine? (Did you remember to squeeze the primer bulb?)

The key here is always to look at the most basic (and therefore the least likely) cause for a problem. Resist the urge to pick up a tool or call a mechanic. Don't panic. Think logically and sequentially. In the majority of cases, you'll find the culprit is not so obvious but so simple as to be truly embarrassing.

2. Has Anything Changed? If your engine ran fine yesterday but shows no signs of life today, ask yourself if anything has been done in the interim. Have you put fuel in it? If so, maybe the fuel is contaminated. Have you or a mechanic worked on it? If the answer is yes, resist the next most common step, which is to say, "But that couldn't have anything to do with it."

For instance, suppose your outboard refuses to start, but it started fine yesterday. The only thing that happened over the last 24 hours is that you changed the fuel filter. But how could that keep your outboard from starting? Retrace your steps and you may find that you inadvertently failed to tighten the filter element and air is being sucked into the fuel line.

3. Does the Engine Have Fuel and Electricity? Suppose you've asked yourself the first two questions and the answers have not revealed a solution. Now it's time to look deeper. First, make sure your engine has what it needs. If you've read this book you know that means clean fuel and air, and a supply of electricity. Once again, as you ask these questions, start with the simplest explanations first and use your God-given logical mind.

Any good mechanic knows there are four basic diagnostic tests to run on an outboard that will almost always reveal the source of the problem. They are:

- Check for spark. If the engine won't turn over, you know your problem is probably on the 12-volt side, and it's probably a dead battery. If is does turn over, your next step is to check for spark. The easiest way to do this is to just pull a spark plug, attach a wire, ground the threads of the spark plug to metal (preferably on the engine block), and have someone crank the engine. You should be able to tell immediately if there's spark. (Remember, only one coil may be out so you should test all spark plugs.)
- Check the condition of the spark plug. If it's wet with fuel you know that fuel is getting to the combustion chamber. If it's dry, you may have a fuel-supply problem. If the plug is really wet, you've probably flooded the engine. First try to start it with the throttle wide open, which will admit more air. If that doesn't work, pull all the plugs, wipe them, clean, and if possible, re-gap them.
- Check the carburetor. Your next step is to make sure fuel is getting to the carburetor. Remove the air intake cover. Unplug the lead from the coil to the distributor so the engine won't start. Look into the carburetor and quickly open the throttle all the way—you can usually do this right at the carburetor by just grabbing the linkage. You should be able to see or smell gasoline. If you can't, chances are no fuel is getting to the carburetor, and it's time to work your way back to the tank. Likely explanations are empty fuel tank, clogged fuel filter, or a clogged anti-siphon valve where the fuel line meets the tank.

Remove this valve with your adjustable wrench, blow it out, and re-insert it.

- Check the compression. If the simple checks fail to reveal a solution, you may have a serious problem. It's time to check the compression with a compression gauge. Low compression is a sign of a broken piston ring or even a cracked cylinder head.

Overheating

One final problem you may someday have to troubleshoot is overheating. Again, the key is to proceed sequentially. First, is water coming out of the telltale or pee hole? If it isn't, first check to see if water is coming in. Believe it or not, many overheating problems are the result of nothing more than a plastic bag wrapped around the water intakes.

If the intakes are clear, the thermostat is the next most likely culprit. But more likely, your raw-water pump is shot. The only real way to check is to pull the lower unit and examine it.

There are literally thousands more questions you could ask in your quest to find the gremlin in your engine. Whatever your predicament, the key is to proceed slowly and logically. Never skip a step. If you can't find the problem by an orderly, sequential process of elimination, then chances are you have a fairly serious problem. That means it's time to quit playing detective and call in an expert.

Index

If you enjoyed *Keep Your Outboard Motor Running*, you might be interested in these books from International Marine:

Boat Trailers and Tow Vehicles: A User's Guide
Steve Henkel

Densely illustrated with Steve Henkel's clear drawings, *Boat Trailers and Tow Vehicles* is packed with information showing adjustment, towing, launching, maintenance, and repair procedures. It describes how to choose the right style and type of trailer for a particular boat and trailering venue; how to choose the best tow vehicle; how to troubleshoot and repair the electrics and wheel bearings; how to correct sway and stability problems while towing; and much more. Detailed appendices include trailer towing regulations by state; trailer towing ratings for cars, vans, and pickups; and a product source list.

"A book like this has been long needed. . . . [It covers] subjects that often take boaters several years to learn. It's a good investment."

—*Trailer Boats*

"The best single source guide I've seen. Commonsense advice, and nicely organized."

—*American Sailor*

"A no-fluff practical primer that can help the trailer boater steer a safe course along the highways to the high seas."

—*Sailing*

Paperbound, 144 pages, 50 illustrations, $14.95. Item No. 028205-6

The Old Outboard Book, Revised and Expanded Edition
Peter Hunn

Now that you've got your outboard running, why not try your hand at finding an older kicker and starting a collection?

The ultimate authority for the old outboard collector is now bigger and better than ever, including the first-ever price guide for collectible outboards built before 1960. Peter Hunn—a lifetime collector of outboard motors—details their history and provides practical advice. A listing of antique outboards will enable anyone to identify a motor and learn its vital statistics. Chapters cover care, simple repair, and operation, and include a comprehensive oil-mix and spark plug chart. Far from being useless, old outboards—particularly those from the mid 1950s—are readily available, easily maintained, and still can be good, reliable performers.

"Even if you are interested in just restoring a motor, the value of the book outweighs its cost. I love it."
—*Eastern and Southeast Boating*

"A primary reference with step-by-step instructions."
—*The Ensign*

"Love old outboard motors? Check out *The Old Outboard Book.*"
—*Motor Boating & Sailing*

"Incredible amount of detail about all those kickers from the past, including an appendix with comprehensive model-year information."
—*WoodenBoat*

Paperbound, 288 pages, 233 illustrations. $19.95. Item No. 031281-8

Getting Started in Powerboating, Second Edition
Captain Bob Armstrong

The first single-source reference guide for powerboaters. Covers how to choose a boat, boat handling, displacement, planing, and semidisplacement hull characteristics, engines and drive trains, and much more. Chapters include invaluable, clearly illustrated discussions on docking, spring lines, and heavy-weather operation. A delivery skipper, private yacht captain, and boat reviewer, Bob Armstrong is well known to readers of *Power and Motoryacht, Boating,* and *Motorboat* magazines.

Paperbound, 224 pages, 198 illustrations, $17.95. Item No. 003095-2

Boat Navigation for the Rest of Us
Captain Bill Brogdon

The first book to teach small-boat navigation the way most people actually navigate, combining electronic aids like radar, GPS, and Loran with commonsense visual piloting and seat-of-the-pants chartwork.

Paperbound, 232 pages, 111 illustrations, $18.95. Item No. 008164-6

How to Order

Call 1-800-822-8158
24 hours a day,
7 days a week
in U.S. and Canada

Mail this coupon to:
McGraw-Hill, Inc.
P.O. Box 182067,
Columbus, OH 43218-2607

Fax your order to:
614-759-3644

EMAIL
70007.1531@COMPUSERVE.COM
COMPUSERVE: GO MH

Shipping and Handling Charges

Order Amount	Within U.S.	Outside U.S.
Less than $15	$3.50	$5.50
$15.00 - $24.99	$4.00	$6.00
$25.00 - $49.99	$5.00	$7.00
$50.00 - $74.49	$6.00	$8.00
$75.00 - and up	$7.00	$9.00

EASY ORDER FORM—
SATISFACTION GUARANTEED

Ship to:

Name _____

Address _____

City/State/Zip _____

Daytime Telephone No. _____

Thank you for your order!

ITEM NO.	QUANTITY	AMT.

Method of Payment:

☐ Check or money order
  enclosed (payable to
  McGraw-Hill)

☐ VISA   ☐ DISCOVER

☐ DINERS CLUB   ☐ MasterCard

Shipping & Handling charge from chart below	
Subtotal	
Please add applicable state & local sales tax	
TOTAL	

Account No. ☐☐☐☐☐☐☐☐☐☐☐☐☐☐☐☐☐☐

Signature _____ Exp. Date _____
    Order invalid without signature

**In a hurry? Call 1-800-822-8158 anytime,
day or night, or visit your local bookstore.**

Code = BC15ZZA